ROBERT WISE

Robert Wise

ROBERT WISE

A Bio-Bibliography

Frank Thompson

Bio-Bibliographies in the Performing Arts, Number 62

GREENWOOD PRESS
Westport, Connecticut • London

Library of Congress Cataloging-in-Publication Data

Thompson, Frank T.
    Robert Wise : a bio-bibliography / Frank Thompson.
       p. cm.—(Bio-bibliographies in the performing arts, ISSN
0892–5550 ; no. 62)
    Includes indexes.
    ISBN 0–313–27812–1 (alk. paper)
    1. Wise, Robert, 1914– . 2. Wise, Robert, 1914– —
Bibliography. 3. Motion picture producers and directors—United
States—Biography. I. Title. II. Series.
PN1998.3.W569T49   1995
791.43′0233′092—dc20
  [B]   94–39512

British Library Cataloguing in Publication Data is available.

Library of Congress Catalog Card Number: 94–39512
ISBN: 0–313–27812–1
ISSN: 0892–5550

First published in 1995

Greenwood Press, 88 Post Road West, Westport, CT 06881
An imprint of Greenwood Publishing Group, Inc.

Printed in the United States of America

∞™

The paper used in this book complies with the
Permanent Paper Standard issued by the National
Information Standards Organization (Z39.48–1984).

10 9 8 7 6 5 4 3 2 1

For
John Andrew Gallagher
My pal, Dan

Contents

Preface

    Scholarship should always begin with enthusiasm. I admired the films of Robert Wise long before I ever began writing about film - indeed, long before I even knew one could take on such a silly profession. My enthusiasm for Wise began when I was about ten years old and saw, in its original release, The Haunting (1963). I still vividly remember everything about that afternoon: the delicious thrill of terror, the utter plausibility of every supernatural occurrence. I remember being particularly gratified to find that all the ghostly goings-on at Hill House did not turn out to be tricks played by unsavory humans - a regular ghost movie cop-out. The Haunting became for me the standard by which all horror films that aimed at being serious and intelligent must be judged. I still feel that way. To me, The Haunting is a work of cinematic art that rewards the closest, most analytical of viewings. It is also a terrific "movie movie" that has the power to make me ten years old again, at least for the space of two hours.

    At around this same time, I was overwhelmed by West Side Story. My parents and friends must have been driven to distraction by my passion for the soundtrack album which I played almost daily until the release of Meet The Beatles introduced a temporary change of direction in my musical tastes (which eventually developed enough to accommodate both West Side Story and The Beatles). In my passion for West Side Story I even, I blush now to admit it, bought a switchblade to be more like a member of The Jets. I daresay I was the only fifth grader in my rural South Carolina grammar school to carry one.

At that age, I never would have made any kind of connection between West Side Story and The Haunting, except, possibly, for the common presence of Russ Tamblyn. Nor would I have drawn any kind of line from those films to others that I had first encountered - and fallen in love with - on television: The Day The Earth Stood Still, Run Silent, Run Deep, I Want To Live!, The Set-Up and - especially - The Body Snatcher. I didn't know then what a film director did and wouldn't have cared much if I had. It was only after a decade had passed, and I was in college in Boston, that I became serious about film study and began to notice that the name Robert Wise showed up on a large number of movies that I liked.

Today, familiar with virtually all of his films, I admire Robert Wise even more. I believe, as many of his critics do, that Wise did not develop a particular style that can be read throughout each of his motion pictures. He was merely a master craftsman, a superb entertainer. But that "merely" is a pretty substantial word. Unlike many of his critics, I don't regard his professionalism as a negative trait. There are a great many film directors who left unique and indelible marks on their works but that doesn't necessarily make them good. If it is difficult to find common themes and recurring motifs in Curse of the Cat People and Star!, who cares? They are both beautifully crafted, interesting, entertaining - and, in the case of Star!, drastically underrated. I will venture to say, in fact, that Robert Wise made very few films that could be called failures as art and/or entertainment, and more than a few of his movies (The Body Snatcher, The Set-Up, The Day The Earth Stood Still, West Side Story) are great.

Commercially, of course, Wise belongs in the pantheon of movie makers. Until the mega-smashes of the George Lucas-Steven Spielberg Seventies, Robert Wise was among the most profitable filmmakers in history. Today, with most of his films available on videocassette and/or laser disc (the preferred video medium for Wise's widescreen films like West Side Story, The Haunting, or Star Trek - The Motion Picture), he reaches audience of ever more vast proportions.

This is not the full-scale biography or critical study that Wise's career deserves. It is intended only as a convenient source of information about the man and his motion pictures. Each film that he worked on -- from his days as Assistant Sound Editor to those films on which he served as Executive Producer -- is represented with the most exhaustive credits possible. In most cases, there are also production notes, critical responses, awards and nominations received, and video sources. When possible I have added comments on each film from Wise himself, culled from several different interviews.

The filmography is followed by a list of articles, interviews and books that deal with Wise and his movies. Where space permits I have quoted from some of the most important articles and books. This will make the bibliography both more valuable for the casual researcher and more enjoyable for the reader. For the serious researcher, this book provides a great jumping off place for locating everything ever written by or about Robert Wise.

Each direct quote throughout this book is identified by the catalog number of the book, article or interview from which the quote was taken. For example, finding [A85] after a quote refers the reader to the "Articles" section of the bibliography and denotes the interview with Wise by John Gallagher in Grand Illusions, Winter, 1977. If the quote comes from an unpublished source, such as my own interviews with Wise directly for this book, the pertinent information appears with the quote itself.

The anecdotal material presented here gives us insight into how Robert Wise brought his many remarkable films to the screen. I hope it also serves a more basic purpose: to inspire the reader to seek out these films (preferably in their original form in a theater) for another look at his impressive body of work. Robert Wise's motion pictures range from blissful escapism to tough, serious explorations of important subjects and themes; his best work contains satisfying elements of both.

As the "bio" in "bio-bibliography" suggests, this book also offers a brief sketch of Robert Wise's life. Sadly, there is not enough space to to cover much more than the bare bones of his career. Wise certainly deserves an in-depth biography, and I hope that some worthy scholar comes along soon to provide one. In the meantime, my fondest wish is that Robert Wise: A Bio-Bibliography will inspire a rediscovery and reexamination of the life and career of one of Hollywood's finest craftsmen and truest gentlemen, Robert Wise.

Acknowledgments

First, of course, my thanks go to Robert Wise, for graciously consenting to read through and correct this manuscript, for submitting to a long interview in New York, mostly concerning <u>The Haunting</u>, and for making all these wonderful films to begin with.

Grateful thanks also to my wife, Claire McCulloch Thompson, for her love and support; to my mother, Geraldine Thompson, for buying me the sound track album to <u>West Side Story</u>, however she may later have regretted it; to my great friend John Gallagher, for granting me free access to the unedited transcripts of his own interviews with Wise; to the friendly and helpful staff of the Margaret Herrick Library of the Motion Picture Academy of Arts and Sciences; to Pete and Molly, my wise dogs; to Selise Eismann and Adele Field of the Directors Guild of America; to Alicia S. Merritt and Emily Okenquist at Greenwood Publishing Group; to Craig R. Covner and Steven Lloyd for providing me with important material; and, most especially, to Thomas W. Holland for his friendship and for assistance far above and beyond the call of duty.

I also wish to thank Kevin Brownlow, John Cocchi, Donna and Mike Durrett, Richard Keenan, C. Jerry Kutner, Scott MacQueen, Tony Malanowski, Dave Miller, Sheryl O'Connell, Gene Phillips S.J., Harry Ringel, Michael Singer, John Tibbetts, Lee Tsiantis and James M. Welsh.

Chronology

1914	Born in Winchester, Indiana, September 10.
1932	Educated in Journalism, Franklin College.
1933	Moves to California to live with brother David. Hired as errand boy, then Assistant Sound Editor at RKO where David works as an accountant.
1934-1938	Promoted from Assistant Sound Editor to Assistant Editor to cutter William Hamilton. Later becomes Hamilton's co-Editor.
1939	Becomes full-fledged Editor, beginning with Garson Kanin's <u>Bachelor Mother</u> and <u>My Favorite Wife</u>.
1941	Edits Orson Welles' <u>Citizen Kane</u> and receives first Academy Award nomination.
1942	Marries Patricia Doyle, May 25. After disastrous previews, is ordered by RKO to cut Welles' <u>The Magnificent Ambersons</u>. He also directs, uncredited, a few new scenes.

1943   Son, Robert Allen, born March 14. Takes over
                direction of Curse of the Cat People when
                original director Gunther von Fritsch falls behind
                schedule.

1944   Assigned by Producer Val Lewton to direct first
                feature: Mademoiselle Fifi.

1949   Directs last film for RKO, The Set-Up.

1950   After one film at Warner Bros., Three Secrets,
                begins tenure at 20th Century-Fox.

1952   With Mark Robson and Theron Warth forms
                Aspen Productions, which releases through
                United Artists.

1953   After one film at Warner Bros., So Big, begins
                tenure at Metro-Goldwyn-Mayer.

1955   Makes Helen of Troy for Warner Bros.

1958   With one film still to go on M-G-M contract,
                moves to United Artists.

                Academy Award nomination as Best Director,
                I Want To Live!

1959   Becomes independent producer for Mirisch
                Corporation.

1961   Shares both Academy Award and Directors
                Guild of America Award for Best Director
                with Jerome Robbins for West Side Story.
                As Producer of West Side Story, takes home a
                second Academy Award for Best Picture.

1963   Becomes independent producer for 20th
                Century-Fox.

1965   Academy Award and Directors Guild of
                America Award as Best Director for The
                Sound of Music. As Producer, also honored

with Best Picture Academy Award.

1966   Receives the Academy of Motion Picture
                    Arts and Sciences Irving G. Thalberg
                    Memorial Academy Award.

1968   Produces The Sergeant, directed by John
                    Flynn. Helps form Film Association for
                    Improvement and Reform (F.A.I.R.). The
                    group later produces King: A Filmed Record
                    (1970), directed by Joseph Mankiewicz and
                    Sidney Lumet.

1970   Forms The Filmakers Group with Mark
                    Robson and Bernard Donnenfeld. Produces
                    The Baby Maker, directed by James Bridges.

1970-76   Appointed to the Council of the National
                    Endowment for the Arts.

1971   Produces the 43rd Annual Academy Awards
                    telecast, April 15.

1971-1975   President of the Directors Guild of
                    America.

1976- present   Chairman of Directors Guild of America's
                    Special Projects Committee.

1977   Married Millicent Franklin, January 29.

1980   Directs The Heart of Hollywood, a
                    promotional film for the Motion Picture
                    Country House and Hospital in Woodland
                    Hills, California.

1982   Elected as Trustee to the American Film
                    Institute.

1983   Receives Honorary Lifetime Membership in the
                    Directors Guild of America.

1985-1987   President of the Motion Picture Academy of
                   Arts and Sciences.

1986   Executive Producer for <u>Wisdom</u>, the first film
                   directed by actor Emilio Estevez.

1988   Receives the D. W. Griffith Award for
                   outstanding achievement and lifetime
                   contribution to film from the Directors
                   Guild of America.

1989   Directs last feature to date, <u>Rooftops</u>.

1991   Receives the Eastman Kodak's Second
                   Century Award.

1992   Receives a National Medal of the Arts from
                   President George Bush.

1993   Honored by a retrospective, "Set-Up in
                   Paradise City" by the Directors Guild of
                   America Special Projects and American
                   Cinematheque, June 11-13.

1994   Appointed a Knight in the Order of Leopold by
                   Belgian King Albert II for lifetime achievement
                   in the film industry and the international
                   acceptance of his motion pictures.

Biographical Sketch

Robert Earl Wise was born on September 10, 1914 in Winchester, Indiana, the second son of Olive (Longnecker) and Earl W. Wise, a meat packer. When Wise was eight years old his family moved to Connersville, Indiana, a town of 12,500 citizens. "I always loved films as a kid and went to them as often as I could afford," Wise said. [A85] But although he regularly attended one of Connersville's three cinemas to enjoy the adventures of childhood heroes like Tom Mix and Douglas Fairbanks, Sr., Wise's first ambition was to be a journalist. After he graduated high school in 1932 he attended Franklin College in Franklin, Indiana for one year.

"I'd gotten a scholarship to go," Wise later said, "and my family managed to scrape together enough money to help get me through the first year, but the second year it looked like it was going to be impossible. It was mid-Depression, my father's business was kind of on the rocks and there wasn't any money for that second year of school." [A85]

Wise's older brother David had gone to California in 1928 and had found work at RKO studios, first as a member of the "labor gang," then working up to an accounting position. When David came home for a vacation that summer of 1933 it was decided that Robert would accompany him back to California.

Wise recalled, "I arrived in Los Angeles in July, 1933 and in the ensuing three or four weeks Dave got me a couple of interviews with department heads at RKO." [A82] The first meeting was with the head of the prop department, who had no work to offer young Wise. The second was with James Wilkinson, head of RKO's editing department.

"He had need of a young eager beaver boy who could work in the shipping room," Wise said, "carry prints up to the projection room for the executives to run and to check prints, store them, patch leader and all those odd jobs." [A85] If the head of the prop department had had a job for Wise, the course of movie history might have been substantially altered.

After working as Wilkinson's "go-fer" for about nine months, Wise became the apprentice for sound editor T. K. Wood. Over the next two years he worked on John Cromwell's Of Human Bondage (1934), George Stevens' Alice Adams (1935), and John Ford's The Informer (1935). He also served as sound effects editor on the Fred Astaire-Ginger Rogers musicals The Gay Divorcee (1934) and Top Hat (1935).

"After I'd done that for a couple of years I looked around and saw men who'd been doing that for fifteen or twenty years," Wise said. "I saw it was a dead end. So I kept after my boss to move me over on the picture side so I could become an assistant film editor and learn film editing, and he was kind enough to do that." [A133]

However, it was also during this period that Wise received his first screen credit. Ernest Schoedsack (who, with Merian Cooper, directed King Kong (1933), among other films) had overshot footage on a South Sea epic he was working on but which was never completed. Wise and Wood, in their spare time, worked some of the footage into a travelogue. "We kept working at it over a period of maybe a year and a half in these lull times," Wise remembered. "Then finally we pulled something together, wrote a commentary for it, showed it to the studio. They gave us, I think, each 500 dollars for our efforts and that was my first screen credit." [A58]

Because RKO was a smaller studio, it presented Wise with better chances of advancing quickly through the ranks. By 1937 he had moved "over to the picture side," assisting film editor William Hamilton on Alfred Santell's Winterset (1936), Gregory La Cava's Stage Door (1937), Mark Sandrich's Carefree (1938) and Santell's Having Wonderful Time (1938).

On working with Hamilton, Wise later recalled, "I used to break the film down, put it on the bench for him to cut. He would stand at the movieola and I would stand at the synch machine and he'd mark while I cut. So he came in one day, we had a small sequence, maybe four or five minutes, and I had the rolls all lined up, all the coverage, and he looked at it and said, 'Why don't you throw that together? Let's see what you can do with it.' First film I'd worked with him. I was a little nervous-like but I stumbled through it somehow and he came down and showed me how it could be improved and all and in about two more pictures I was doing all the first cutting in the room, and he would be up on the set with the director. He'd come down and look at the sequence and improve it, and the last three films I did with him, I was doing so much of the work, he insisted I share credit." [A133]

Hamilton considered Wise his co-editor on La Cava's Fifth Avenue Girl (1939), H.C. Potter's The Story of Vernon and Irene Castle (1939) and William Dieterle's The Hunchback of Notre Dame (1939), the first feature for which he received screen credit.

In 1939, Wise became an editor himself, beginning with Garson Kanin's Bachelor Mother. "Because Gar was new to films," Wise said, "he always wanted the editor on the set with him to help him with the camera setups, to be sure he got enough coverage. So for Bachelor Mother and My Favorite Wife, my assistant Mark Robson was down in the editing room doing the first cuts while I worked with Gar up on the set." [A85] Wise found working with Kanin "invaluable" training for his eventual career as a director.

A more interesting -- and controversial -- encounter with a director, however, was still to come. In 1941, Orson Welles chose Wise to cut Welles' first feature film, Citizen Kane. "Orson had been shooting scenes that were thought to be tests for the picture," Wise recalled, "but they turned out to be sequences [used] in the final picture. Orson had an older editor assigned to him for those tests and evidently he was not too happy with that particular assignment. I was roughly Orson's age, so I went down to Pathe in Culver City and met him; we had a chat between setups. He liked me and wanted me to come on the picture." [A85]

Citizen Kane became a landmark in the American cinema and Wise received his first Academy Award nomination for editing it. Welles immediately began work on his next film, an adaptation of Booth Tarkington's The Magnificent Ambersons and Wise, again, signed on as editor. As post-production on Ambersons began, Welles left for South America to make a documentary It's All True. He supervised Wise's editing through a series of epic-length cables but, apart from three days in a Florida animation studio, the two could not fully collaborate on the editing of the film. After a disastrous preview of Ambersons in which the audience ridiculed the film and filled out damning reports on the opinion cards, RKO had Wise cut the film and direct a few bridging sequences. While the scenes marked Wise's first experience as a director, Welles complained bitterly for the rest of his life that Ambersons had been "mutilated."

Wise continues, however, to defend RKO's version of The Magnificent Ambersons. "There have been statements that Orson thought the film was ruined by the studio and by us, but I say that is wrong; we can't have ruined it because it has come down through the years as a classic in its own right. I would be the first to admit that as a work of art it was a much better film in its original form, no question about it." [A57; see Magnificent Ambersons - Notes: in Filmography]

For the next two years, Wise edited less significant RKO pictures like Tim Whelan's Seven Days Leave (1942) and Richard Wallace's Bombardier (1943). He even got another crack at directing when a few scenes in Wallace's The Fallen Sparrow (1943) had to be re-shot.

Wise's urge to become a director was getting stronger and, in September, 1943, he got his chance. Editing a psychological horror film, Curse of the Cat People, for producer Val Lewton, Wise was asked to take over with director Gunther von Fritsch, formerly a documentarian, was fired.

Wise remembered, "Gunther was a lovely guy and doing a good job but very, very slowly. He couldn't seem to pick his pace up. He got so far behind and they couldn't seem to make him go faster - these were limited budget films. They finally just had to take him off. They told me on a Saturday noon they wanted me to direct Monday morning. I showed some reluctance to do this because it was awkward. I was working with the man. I expressed this reluctance to Lewton and Sid Rogell, who was executive producer of the RKO B unit. [Sid] said, 'Listen, somebody else is going to be on that stage directing Monday. Now it could be you or it could be Joe Blow, but it's not going to be Gunther. What do you want to do?' And since I had been at them to give me the chance to direct, I had to take it." [A90] RKO announced, falsely, that von Fritsch had been drafted.

Lewton immediately assigned Wise to direct a feature of his own, an adaptation of two Guy de Maupassant stories called Mademoiselle Fifi. Called "a brave yet delicate chamber film" by Lewton scholar Joel E. Siegel [B65], the film is an historical drama set in the Franco-Prussian War - a rare non-horror film from Lewton but one which perfectly reflects the producer's obsession with accurately portraying a particular moment in time. Lewton was, Wise said, "an exceptional man, highly cultured, well-read, a writer himself, a man of great taste and great imagination, a really creative producer." [A85]

Wise's next assignment, The Body Snatcher (1945), was a more typical Lewton enterprise, but it remains one of Wise's best motion pictures, and one of the finest and subtlest horror films ever made. Based on the short story by Robert Louis Stevenson (who in turn based his story on the infamous grave robbers Burke and Hare), The Body Snatcher stars Boris Karloff, Henry Daniell and, in a small role, Bela Lugosi. The film is set in 1831 Edinburgh, where the director of a medical school (Daniell) must deal with a grave robber (Karloff) to obtain cadavers for study. Again, Lewton and Wise beautifully recreate a time and place, all the more astonishing given the obvious limits of their budget. The horror, typically of Lewton, is more suggested than shown and is generally more psychological than physical. Even so, the climax, which features a runaway carriage, a driving rainstorm and a vengeful corpse, is among the cinema's most terrifying moments.

After A Game of Death (1945), a remake of The Most Dangerous Game (1932), Criminal Court (1946; "just one of those B pictures one does under contract" [A57]), Born to Kill (1947), a sordid film noir starring Lawrence Tierney, and Mystery in Mexico (1948; "I had no big drive to do it at all" [A57]), Wise directed a superb, moody Western, Blood on the Moon (1948), starring Robert Mitchum. Eschewing the expansive outdoor quality of most Westerns, Blood on the Moon was filmed mostly on interior sets with ceilings (the Citizen Kane influence), and low-key, moody lighting. It has, writes historian William K. Everson, "some of the starkness and austerity of the William S. Hart Westerns." [B32]

With this excellent film under his belt, Wise was poised for the work that would bring him the first real critical acclaim of his career: The Set-Up (1949). Based on a narrative poem by Joseph Moncure March, written in 1929, The Set-Up told of a boxer who is told by the mob to throw a fight. When he refuses and wins the match, the mobsters beat him and break his hands. Beautifully acted by Robert Ryan, the boxer is a decent, slightly dull-witted palooka whose wife (Audrey Totter) desperately wants him to quit before boxing costs him his life. The boxing sequences are among the most powerful put on film and Wise approached them as if staging a dance.

Boxer John Indrisano staged the fight sequences (a job he repeated on Somebody Up There Likes Me and The Sand Pebbles) for the camera. "I call it choreography," Wise said. "At the old YMCA in Hollywood, they had a ring up there, and I would go in on a Saturday - before we started shooting - and see what they were doing, make some suggestions, fewer punches, more, whatever. Gradually build it that way. Then when we shot it, we would just do it in sections, with three cameras on each fight: one camera to cover the whole ring, another one to be in tighter...and another one, just a wild camera, for those little pieces, the spray flying and all that. [The cameraman] was up close with a little hand-held camera." [A133]

The Set-Up was Wise's last film at RKO and he left for a three year, non-exclusive contract with 20th Century-Fox, after making a single melodrama, Three Secrets (1950), at Warner Bros. His first Fox film was a rousing Western, set in the Indian territories during the time of the Civil War, Two Flags West (1950). This was followed up by an underrated thriller, House on Telegraph Hill (1951) and then by one of Wise's greatest, most enduring works, The Day The Earth Stood Still (1951).

This science fiction classic concerns Klaatu, a delegate from another planet who arrives on Earth to warn that nuclear buildup will someday destroy the entire universe. Although many critics have seen Klaatu as a Christ figure (his earth name is "Mr. Carpenter", he brings a message of peace and is killed for it, then rises from the dead), Wise has said that he meant nothing of the kind. He was, however," quite adamant about the anti-militarist, anti-nuclear themes of the film. "I wish the message could have gotten out more clearly around the world, to the powers that be, but I'm afraid that's too much to hope for," Wise said. [A133; see The Day The Earth Stood Still - Notes in Filmography]

In 1952, Wise teamed with two old RKO cronies, director Mark Robson and producer Theron Warth, to form Aspen Productions. The company didn't last long, eventually producing only two films: Wise's Captive City (1952) and Robson's Return to Paradise (1953). Captive City was an expose film, shot entirely on location in Nevada, about the insidious spread of organized crime. Wise wrote at the time [A2], "In making a crime movie away from Hollywood it has become custom for the press agent to frame a story that the director's life has been threatened. I can't say that mine was or wasn't, but I did receive two anonymous telephone calls suggesting that I call the picture off. These could have been the practical jokes of the actors or crew.

"I do know, however, that the Syndicate is aware of our Captive City. After our location work was completed, the police official told me that he had been visited regularly by various underworld menials, small time hoods who probably had been told to find out what the picture was all about." [A2] Wise took a print of Captive City to Washington, D.C. to show to the crime commission of Senator Estes Kefauver, who agreed to endorse the film and appear in its epilogue.

Next was a change of pace - and Wise's only full-fledged comedy - Something for the Birds (1952) in which Patricia Neal, who also starred in The Day The Earth Stood Still, lobbies Congress for the endangered California Condor.

Wise completed his Fox contract with a pair of World War II dramas, Destination Gobi (1953) and The Desert Rats (1953), starring James Mason and Richard Burton. The film, concerning the 1941 siege of Tobruk, was a follow-up to Henry Hathaway's The Desert Fox (1951) which also starred Mason as Field Marshall Rommel of the Afrika Corps. Destination Gobi is notable as Wise's first color film and

The Desert Rats received an Academy Award nomination for Richard Murphy's screenplay.

The highly-praised business drama Executive Suite (1954) introduced Wise to the gloss of Metro-Goldwyn-Mayer. French critic Jean-Pierre Coursodan writes that the film, "may be, in terms of pure craftsmanship, his masterpiece. Executive Suite may paint a somewhat naive, shcematized, or romanticized picture of power struggles in the world of big business; still it is one of the more complex and dramatically satisfying ever presented by the movies." [B20] The film won many awards and was nominated for many more. It firmly established Wise as one of Hollywood's top directors.

In later years Wise recalled with satisfaction the pleasure of working with the large, ensemble cast of Executive Suite, including William Holden, Barbara Stanwyck, Fredric March, June Allyson and others. But he didn't have similarly pleasant memories of his next film, the epic Helen of Troy. "[It] is my first and last venture in spectacle," Wise said later. "It was a genre of film that seemed to be coming on and I wanted to prove to myself that I could do that kind of big spectacle. I didn't enjoy doing it really. It was massive and unwieldy." [A85] Wise replaced veteran director Michael Curtiz on the film and was, in turn, assisted by another veteran, Raoul Walsh, who pitched in to shoot some second unit footage. Filmed in the new anamorphic CinemaScope process, Helen of Troy was praised by critics for its visual power but panned for the poor script and wooden acting. [see Helen of Troy - Notes in Filmography]

His next film, however, was almost universally praised. It was the story of boxer Rocky Graziano, Somebody Up There Likes Me (1956). Paul Newman played Graziano, a role originally to have been played by James Dean, who died on September 30, 1955. Wise recalled, "Newman...had only made two or three films and he was very tied to the stage technique. He was a marvelous professional and fine to work with, but I found that if he came in with a suggestion or idea and I didn't like it, it would gnaw at him; I wouldn't get his full shot. So I found it simpler most times when he came up with an idea, I'd let him try it out. Sometimes it would work, other times it wouldn't. But he would get it out of his system and it wouldn't bother him anymore." [A85]

"I hadn't really been very strong for having Pier Angeli in the show," Wise said. "Graziano's wife was not actually Italian, certainly not a native born Italian, so I rather resisted the idea of somebody with an accent, but we simply couldn't seem to find a person with just the qualities we thought were right. [I thought] she did such an awfully good job in the film, she seemed very real, very warm." [A61]

Somebody Up There Likes Me was Wise's most successful film of the period, catapulting Paul Newman to stardom. The film also introduced Steve McQueen in a small role; McQueen would later give one of his finest performances for Wise in The Sand Pebbles (1966). Wise elected to follow this powerful biography with a frothy musical comedy This Could Be The Night (1957), with a witty script by Isobel Lennart. Critics mentioned the film's Damon Runyonesque flavor, but both they and audiences found the film amusing. Jean Simmons starred both in this film and in Wise's next, a World War II soap opera, Until They Sail (1957).

With one picture still to go on his M-G-M contract, Wise moved over to United Artists, a company which was to release some of his most successful films. The first was the World War II submarine drama Run Silent, Run Deep (1958) starring Burt Lancaster and Clark Gable. "Gable was an old pro," Wise recalled. "He was very punctual, very professional. He was always there in the morning ahead of time and ready to go at 9:00. But at 5:00, that was it. He absolutely refused to work later. Of course he was in his late fifties then and would get tired at the end of the day and felt he couldn't give his best or look his best. But he had no phony temperament; very much a gentleman and a professional. I had the highest regard and respect for him." [A85]

Wise told the story of convicted murderess Barbara Graham in I Want To Live! (1958), a powerful diatribe against capital punishment. The film's grim, almost documentary air came from Wise's intense commitment to portraying the execution as realistically as possible. He visited San Quentin prison, taking copious pictures from which the accurate sets would be replicated and talking with the Warden and prison guards about the procedures of taking a life in the gas chamber. Feeling the need to truly understand this horrible experience, Wise even witnessed an execution himself.

Susan Hayward's performance won her an Academy Award and several other honors and I Want To Live! remains a stunning experience -- despite the fact that the film's claims for Graham's innocence have been fairly thoroughly refuted by history. For Wise, her guilt or innocence is almost irrelevant to the message of the film. "Nobody should have to go through that kind of torture," he said. "We wanted to make the film an indictment of capital punishment by just showing what it is like to die in the chamber, how meaningless it is, how little it resolves." [A85]

Wise is sometimes remembered only for blockbusters like West Side Story and The Sound of Music but throughout his career he retained the taste for low budget films with a point that he cultivated at RKO. Between I Want To Live! and West Side Story is one of these,

Odds Against Tomorrow (1989), produced by and starring Harry Belafonte. Critic Richard Roud called it "a rather meditative, downbeat film about a robbery, very stylishly shot in a frosty winter New York." [B59]

Shot on location in a small town in upstate New York and in the Gold Medal Studios in the Bronx, Odds Against Tomorrow is reminiscent of Stanley Kramer's The Defiant Ones (1958) with its themes of racial tension. In fact, the ending of the novel by William P. McGivern struck Wise as being far too similar to that of Kramer's film. "And I thought, we can't do the same thing," Wise said. "We have to show the other side of the coin, destroy them at the end, so we can say, 'Hate destroys. Look at what happened to these guys -- the hatred they had killed them.' So that's what we did." [A133]

The script of Odds Against Tomorrow is credited to John O. Killens and, from I Want To Live!, Nelson Gidding, Wise's most frequent writing collaborator. But another writer had a major hand in the screenplay as well: blacklisted writer/director Abraham Polonsky.

While in New York, completing post-production on Odds Against Tomorrow Wise was approached to direct the screen version of the hit musical West Side Story. He accepted, eventually co-directing with Jerome Robbins, the creative mind behind the stage version. West Side Story became the pivotal point in Wise's career, turning him, in writer C. Jerry Kutner's words, from "a respected genre craftsman" to "a Hollywood Superstar." [A134]

West Side Story won ten Academy Awards (plus a special Oscar for Robbins), including Best Picture and Best Director, and a host of other awards. It was also an overwhelming hit at the box-office. Together with the phenomenal success of The Sound of Music in 1965, West Side Story placed Wise in the pantheon of the cinema's most successful filmmakers. [see West Side Story - Notes in Filmography]

After the big-budget production of West Side Story, Wise scaled down for an adaptation of the stage comedy Two For The Seesaw. Essentially a two character film, Seesaw concerns a Mid-Western lawyer (Robert Mitchum) who becomes involved with a kooky New Yorker (Shirley MacLaine). The Hollywood Reporter's James Powers called the film, "a bittersweet romance with virtually no distracting elements...directed with humanity and delicacy." [October 30, 1962]

Owing one film to Metro-Goldwyn-Mayer from his old contract, Wise approached the studio with the idea of filming Shirley Jackson's ghost novel "The Haunting of Hill House." After finding that the film could be made relatively cheaply in England, M-G-M agreed and Wise directed one of his finest works, The Haunting (1963), starring Julie Harris, Claire Bloom, Russ Tamblyn and Richard Johnson. The film was produced at the M-G-M Borehamwood Studios outside London and at Ettington Hall, an eighteenth-century manor house near Stratford-on-Avon. The cast and the crew actually lived in the house during part of the production. The real interior, however, wasn't as creepy ("There are no right angles anywhere," says one character) as the sets; they were built on the soundstage.

The Haunting is a return to Wise's roots in the Val Lewton RKO horror unit. "I loved doing those films with Lewton," Wise said. "I learned much from him and one of the reasons I got caught up in wanting to do The Haunting was the need to return to that kind of film - that kind of thriller show that I had started my directing career on." [A85; see The Haunting - Notes in Filmography]

Wise then began planning another blockbuster, The Sand Pebbles, a drama about an American gunboat in war-torn China, circa 1926. The Mirisch Company was set to produce the film but they became concerned about the budget and, in 1964, withdrew. Wise took The Sand Pebbles over to 20th Century-Fox. Fox was interested but had more pressing matters to attend to. Veteran director William Wyler had just withdrawn from the big-budget musical The Sound of Music (1965) and Fox asked Wise to take Wyler's place.

Wise accepted in exchange for a percentage of the profits and an agreement from Fox to finance The Sand Pebbles. It was an immensely profitable deal for Wise, but if Fox felt at all uneasy about making it, all such doubts vanished when The Sound of Music quickly became the top money maker in Hollywood history, grossing an incredible $100 million in the first two years of release.

"I thought it was a chance to do a different kind of musical," Wise said, "one that could entertain all kinds of people and still had something serious to say." [A85] Most of the reviews were mixed at best but The Sound of Music won numerous awards. More importantly it became a member of the rarest society: movies that are truly beloved.

With the astonishing success of The Sound of Music behind him, Wise was then able to take up The Sand Pebbles (1966) again. Fox spent $12 million on the production and Wise filmed it in Taiwan and Hong Kong. An arduous production, The Sand Pebbles had to withstand terrible weather, uncooperative Communist officials and at least one riot but it was rewarded with eight Oscar nominations, respectable box-office and good reviews. At that year's Academy Awards ceremony, Wise received the coveted Irving G. Thalberg, the Academy's highest honor, for consistent excellence and achievement.

Wise and The Sound of Music star Julie Andrews teamed again for an epic biography of musical star Gertrude Lawrence called Star! (1968). Although hopes were high that the golden team could repeat the success of Music, Star! failed miserably at the box office. Audiences' tastes had shifted markedly in the three years since Music but Wise was at a loss to explain why Star! bombed so completely. "I guess audiences couldn't accept Julie playing that kind of character," he said. "It was a different range of emotion and feelings, a lady who can get drunk and high." [A85] Star! was later cut by nearly an hour and rereleased as Those Were the Happy Times in 1969. The film fared no better with its new title and length. In 1990, Star! was restored to its original length and played to enthusiastic audiences in several major cities.

Despite the failure of Star!, Wise remained one of the most powerful men in show business. In 1968 he planned to produce a television special with bawdy cinema legend Mae West. The network, however, got cold feet about the project and pulled the plug. During this same period, Wise, acting as executive producer, oversaw two young directors' first films: John Flynn's The Sergeant (1968) and James Bridges' The Baby Maker (1970).

In January, 1970 Wise formed The Filmakers Group with Bridges, Mark Robson and ex-Paramount vice president Bernard Donnenfeld. His first production for the group was an adaptation of Michael Crichton's "science fact" novel about germ warfare and a deadly virus from outer space, The Andromeda Strain (1971). For the first time, Wise had final cut on a motion picture and the film was praised by critics for its realistic scientific atmosphere and state-of-the-art special effects by Douglas Trumbull (2001: A Space Odyssey).

The Filmakers Group was an idea that never quite caught on. "We formed it hoping that we could get together some independent financing for our films and not have to be tied to the studios," Wise said. "But that turned out to be more of a dream. We got money, but the people with the money wanted so much of a piece of the company that we felt we were better off going back to the studios to make our deals with them." [A90] The Filmakers Group produced Mark Robson's Happy Birthday, Wanda June (1971) and Earthquake (1974) and Wise's Two People (1971) and The Hindenburg (1975). "Of course," Wise said, "the one big winner out of it was Earthquake." [A137]

Two People, filmed entirely on location in Marrakech, Casablanca, Paris and New York, starred Peter Fonda and Lindsay Wagner. It made virtually no impact at the box office and remains one of Wise's least known, and least effective, films. His next film, however, was one of his most ambitious: The Hindenburg (1975).

The Hindenburg tells the dramatic story of the German zeppelin which mysteriously burst into flames after a transatlantic flight in 1937. Although still unsolved, many believe that the tragedy was caused by a bomb placed on board; certainly this is the film's solution. George C. Scott plays a Gestapo officer, disgusted by the increasing atrocities of the Third Reich, who is placed on board the airship to investigate bomb threats.

Critics derided its Grand Hotel-like script but no one could deny the extraordinary power of the film's final sequences in which newly shot footage (in black and white) were intercut with actual newsreel footage of the burning Hindenburg. Wise exhaustively researched the period and, with the amazing visual effects work of Albert Whitlock, recreated the Art Deco elegance of this flying palace. The main problem with The Hindenburg is that, because the ending is a foregone conclusion, it is almost impossible to get any genuine suspense into the plot. As Scott and fellow Gestapo official Roy Thinnes investigate the various passengers and crew, and uncover one red herring after another, the general effect is of time wasted. [see The Hindenburg - Notes in Filmography]

Audrey Rose (1977) was taken by many critics as just another variation on The Exorcist (1974). But this morbid and fascinating exploration of reincarnation is among the most underrated films of Wise's career. A fine performance by twelve year-old Susan Swift, is at the heart of this supernatural mystery story. Variety's reviewer found that the "script does a good job in interpolating the necessary philosophical and metaphysical explanations of reincarnation without being overly didactic or tediously expository. The bits and pieces of key spiritual info are motivated by physical action and happenings which will keep the attention of the popcorn trade. Hence, the film works on high and low intelligence levels." [April 6, 1977]

A big-budget, special effects-laden movie version of Gene Roddenberry's television series Star Trek was Wise's next film. Star Trek -- The Motion Picture (1979) reunited the cast of the cult series, William Shatner, Leonard Nimoy and others. While it was generally savaged by the critics, it was popular enough with the public to spawn five more sequels. "It was tough going," Wise said. "That was not one my most pleasant experiences - not because of the actors. Shooting was fine. Working with Bill and Leonard and Nichelle [Nichols] and George [Takei] and all the rest, they were all fine. But it's difficult when you're rewriting all the way through." [A134]

Over the next decade, Wise only directed one film, a promotional piece for the Motion Picture Country House and Hospital in Woodland Hills, California called The Heart of Hollywood (1980). But he did not remain idle; he continued to chair the Special Projects Committee of the Directors Guild of America, served as a Trustee to the American Film Institute and served as president of the Academy of Motion Picture Arts and Sciences from 1985-87.

Always eager to help out young filmmakers, Wise served as Executive Producer for the first directorial effort by actor Emilio Estevez, Wisdom (1986). Some observers claim that Wise also directed a major portion of the film, a charge that Wise denies emphatically.

In 1988, he received the Directors Guild's D. W. Griffith Award for outstanding lifetime achievement. But this was not a late honor for a retired filmmaker. Even while accepting the award, Wise was at work on his next feature, Rooftops (1989).

Rooftops seems in some ways an updated take on West Side Story, taking place among a violent youth subculture in New York City. The kids in Rooftops express themselves by "combat dancing," which was created for the film. Wise told The Hollywood Reporter, "We wanted a dance that would ... be an outlet for their emotions. We came up with this idea of doing a dance that would be, in a sense, like fighting, but in a dance form." [March 16, 1989]

The critics didn't like Rooftops; the L. A. Herald Examiner's Andy Klein wrote that the film "provides all the immediate pleasures that might appeal to undemanding teenagers. For anyone born prior to 1969, even its visceral satisfactions are likely to wear thin quickly." [March 20, 1989] The public didn't take much notice, either. Rooftops is, at this writing, Robert Wise's last film.

****

Critics, particularly those who grew out of the auteur furor of the Fifties and Sixties, tend to distrust versatility. They believe, perhaps, that an artist who proves adept at many genres can have no true personal style. They also distrust financial success, preferring to champion struggling Poverty Row artists like Edgar G. Ulmer, who made interesting pictures for minuscule budgets, to phenomenally popular entertainers like Steven Spielberg, whose films have earned more than the gross national product of some countries.

The career of Robert Wise has lasted long enough for him to find himself admired by some, despised by others; sometimes admired, then despised. Auteurists cling to his dark, gritty work at RKO and reject his blockbusters of the Sixties: Born to Kill good, The Sound of Music bad.

In fact, a good hard look at Wise's canon shows that the experimental maverick of the Forties was alive and well into the Eighties. The Hindenburg, for all its failings as drama, relentlessly pushes the limits of screen techniques, creating a real, believable world out of little more than paintings, models and camera effects. The bravura camera movement of West Side Story and the bold, deep focus chiaroscuro of The Haunting reveal both a young filmmaker's audaciousness and an experienced pro's accomplishment.

"I don't think there's necessarily a contradiction between a good movie artistically and a good movie commercially," Wise has said. "I am very much a believer in not catering to the audience, like television does so much, but you must consider the audience ... realize that it is being made not just for your own subjective, personal taste but for millions of people out there. It seems to me the more appeal the movie has to the great mass of people, without sacrificing artistic quality, the more effect your theme will have. If you make it so personal, so to yourself, so special that very few people go to see it, then you really haven't punched over what you have to say. The potency of the theme of your film is only as good as the number of people who see it."

Filmography

The following filmography attempts to depict the whole of Robert Wise's career in film from his first job as apprentice sound editor at RKO to his most recent motion pictures as director and producer. The credits are, in each case, as complete as possible.

The credits were drawn from a number of sources: original call sheets, press books, reference books and the films themselves. I would here like to acknowledge the invaluable assistance of John Cocchi in compiling this filmography.

Assistant Sound Editor

F1   OF HUMAN BONDAGE (1934).

RKO-Radio. A Pandro S. Berman Production.

Director: John Cromwell. Screenplay: Lester Cohen. Based upon the 1915 novel by W. Somerset Maugham; Dialogue: Ann Coleman; Editor: William Morgan. Sound Editor: T. K. Wood; Assistant Directors: J. Dewey Starkey and Kenneth Holmes; 2nd Camera: Bob DeGrasse; Photographic Effects: Vernon Walker; Gaffer: Guy Gilman; Second Camera Assistant: George Diskant; Art Direction: Van Nest Polglase and Carroll Clark; Costumes: Walter Plunkett; Wardrobe: Ethel Beach and Tommy Clark; Music: Max Steiner; Recording Engineer: Clem Portman; Assistant Recording Engineer: Eddie Harmon; Makeup: Sam Kaufman; Hairstyles: Dot Carlson; Unit Manager: J. R. Crone; Script Clerk: Betty Goode; Grip: Sam Redding; Propman: George Gabe;

Best Boy: George Marquenne; Still Photographer: Alex Kahle. 83 minutes.

Cast: Bette Davis (Mildred Rogers); Leslie Howard (Philip Carey); Frances Dee (Sally Athelny); Reginald Owen (Thrope Athelny); Kay Johnson (Norah); Reginald Denny (Harry Griffiths); Alan Hale (Emile Miller); Reginald Sheffield (Cyril Dunsford); Desmond Roberts (Dr. Jacobs); Frank Baker (Policeman); Douglas Gordon (Hawker); Frank Mills (Chimney sweep); Ma Curly (Charwoman); Tom Hughes (Englishman); Nat Neahan (Slim); Al Sullivan (Jimmy Gray); Ray Atchley (J. Murphy); Madline Wilson (Girl); Frankie Grandetta (Newsboy); Irene Rich (Baby); Sally Sage (Double); Charles Coleman (Tempe Pigott); Pat Somerset, Billy Mills, Harry Allen, Frank Schwab, Byron Fitzpatrick, James Casey, Adrian Rosley.

Notes: Of Human Bondage was re-made in 1946, starring Paul Henreid and Eleanor Parker and in 1964 with Laurence Harvey and Kim Novak.

Video Availability: Nostalgia Family Video.

F2   THE GAY DIVORCEE (1934).

RKO-Radio. A Pandro S. Berman Production.

Director: Mark Sandrich. Editor: William Hamilton. Sound Editor: T.K. Wood; Assistant Director: Argyle Nelson; 2nd Assistant Directors: Ray Lissner and Ivan Thomas; Screenplay:George Marion Jr., Dorothy Yost and Edward Kaufman; Additional Dialogue: H. W. Hanemann, Stanley Rauh and Robert Benchley; Based on the 1932 musical play The Gay Divorce, book by Dwight Taylor, music and lyrics by Cole Porter, musical adaptation by Kenneth Webb and Samuel Hoffenstein; Director of Photography: David Abel; Camera Operator: Joseph Biroc; Assistant Camera: Willard Barth and Clifford Stine; Additional Photography: Bill Williams; Special Effects: Vernon Walker; Art Direction: Van Nest Polglase and Carroll Clark; Costumes: Walter Plunkett; Wardrobe: Claire Cramer; Music: Max Steiner; Dance Director: Hermes Pan; Dance Ensemble staged by: Dave Gould; Sound: Hugh McDowell, Jr.; Music Recording: Murray Spivack and P.J. Faulkner Jr.; Technical Director: Peter Croft; Production Manager: J. R. Crone; Script Clerk: Trudy Wellman; Electrician: James Vianna; Grip: Jim Davis; Propman: Thomas Little; Projectionist: Bill Hamberry; Still Photographer: Fred Hendrickson; Stand-in for Fred Astaire: Harry Cornbleth; Stand-in

for Ginger Rogers: Marie Osborne; Stand-in for Alice Brady: Madeline
Wilson. 107 minutes.

Songs: "Night and Day" by Cole Porter; "The Continental" and
"A Needle in a Haystack" music by Con Conrad, lyrics by Herb
Magidson; "Don't Let It Bother You" and "Let's K-nock K-neez" music
by Harry Revel, lyrics by Mack Gordon.

Cast: Fred Astaire (Guy Holden); Ginger Rogers (Mimi Glossop);
Alice Brady (Aunt Hortense); Edward Everett Horton (Egbert "Pinky"
Fitzgerald); Erik Rhodes (Rodolfo Tonetti); Eric Blore (Waiter); William
Austin (Cyril Glossop); Charles Coleman (The Valet); Lillian Miles
(Guest); Betty Grable (Guest/performer in "Let's K-nock K-nees"
number); Charles Dunbar, Frank Mills, William Wanger, J. G. McMahon
(Waiters); Jack Grant, Cy Clegg (Porters); Charles Hall (Messenger); E.
E. Clive (Chief Inspector); Cyril Thornton (Second Inspector); Les
Goodwins (Baggage Man); Ronnie Rondell, Bryce Wyndham, Ted
Oliver, Art Jarrett, Finis Barton, Sonny Ray, Sidney Jarvis, Flo Wicks,
Norman Ainsley, Jimmy Aubrey.

Awards: Academy Award, Best Song "The Continental."
Academy Award nominations: Best Interior Decoration, Best Picture,
Best Sound, Best Score.

Video Availability: Turner Home Video.

F3 ALICE ADAMS (1935).

RKO-Radio. A Pandro S. Berman Production.

Director: George Stevens; Director of Photography: Robert de
Grasse; Screenplay: Dorothy Yost, Mortimer Offner and Jane Murfin;
Based upon the 1921 novel by Booth Tarkington; Editor: William
Hamilton; Sound Editor: T.K. Wood; Art Director: Van Nest Polglase;
Associate Art Director: Perry Ferguson; Costumes: Walter Plunkett;
Music Director: Roy Webb; Sound: D. A. Cutler; Unit Manager: J. R.
Crone; Script Clerk: Ann Coleman; Research: Elizabeth McGaffey;
Assistant Directors: Edward Killy, Dick Green and James Harnet;
Location Manager: Herb Hist; Assistant Location Manager: A. D.
Schroeder; Stand-ins: Patsy Doyle, Russell Beach, John Huffner and Bill
Van Vleck; Director's Staff: Jane Loring. 95 minutes.

Song: "I Can't Waltz Alone" lyrics by Dorothy Fields, music by Max Steiner.

Cast: Katharine Hepburn (Alice Adams); Fred MacMurray (Arthur Russell); Fred Stone (Virgil Adams); Evelyn Venable (Mildred Palmer); Frank Albertson (Walter Adams); Ann Shoemaker (Mars. Adams); Charley Grapewin (J. A. Lamb); Grady Sutton (Frank Dowling); Hedda Hopper (Mrs. Palmer); Jonathan Hale (Mr. Palmer); Hattie McDaniel (Malena Burns); Janet McLeod (Henrietta Lamb); Virginia Howell (Mrs. Dowling); Zeffie Tilbury (Mrs. Dresser); Ella McKenzie (Ella Dowling); Frank Ward (Kid Herman); George Warrington (Frank Yaconelli); Monte Carter, Margaret Morris.

Awards: Academy Award nominations for Best Actress (Hepburn) and Best Picture. National Board of Review Awards: 10 Best Films of the Year.

Video Availability: Nostalgia Family Video.

F4   THE INFORMER (1935).

RKO-Radio. A John Ford Production.

Associate Producer: Cliff Reid; Director: John Ford; Screenplay: Dudley Nichols; Contributor to Treatment: Liam O'Flaherty; Based upon the 1925 novel by Liam O'Flaherty; Director of Photography: Joseph H. August; Art Director: Van Nest Polglase; Set Decorator: Julia Heron; Editor: George Hively; Costumes: Walter Plunkett; Music: Max Steiner; Sound: Hugh McDowell, Jr.; Sound Editor: T.K. Wood; Research: Elizabeth McGaffey; Assistant Directors: Ed O'Fearna and Eddie Donahue; Press Agent: S. Barrett McCormick. 97 minutes.

Cast: Victor McLaglen (Gypo Nolan); Preston Foster (Dan Gallagher); Heather Angel (Mary McPhillip); Margot Grahame (Katie Madden); Wallace Ford (Frankie McPhillip); Una O'Connor (Mrs. McPhillip); J. M. Kerrigan (Terry); Joseph Sauers (Barteley Mulholland); Neil Fitzgerald (Tommy Connor); Donald Meek (Pat Mulligan); D'Arcy Corrigan (The Blind Man); Leo McCabe (Donahue); Gaylord Pendleton (Daley); Francis Ford (Flynn); May Boley (Madame Betty) Grizelda Harvey (The Lady); Denis O'Dea (Street Singer); Clyde Cook (Man at Madame Betty's); J. Farrell MacDonald (Man in Street); Major Sam Harris, Earle Fox (British Officers); James Murray, Frank Moran, Arthur

McLaglen, Barlowe Borland.

Awards: Academy Awards: Best Actor (McGlaglen), Best Director, Best Screenplay, Best Score. Academy Award Nominations: Best Picture, Best Film Editing. New York Film Critics: Best Picture, Best Director. National Board of Review: 10 Best Films of the Year.

Video Availability: VidAmerica Inc., Baker and Taylor Video.

F5   TOP HAT (1935).

RKO-Radio. A Pandro S. Berman Production.

Director: Mark Sandrich. Editor: William Hamilton. Sound Editor: T.K. Wood; Assistant Director: C. C. Thompson. Harry D'Arcy, Richard Green and Kenneth Holmes; Screenplay: Dwight Taylor and Allan Scott; Story: Dwight Taylor; Adaptation: Karl Noti; Contributor to Treatment: Ben Holmes; Contributor to Screenplay Construction: Ralph Spence; Based on the 1911 play The Girl Who Dared (or A Scandal in Budapest) by Alexander Farago and Aladar Laszlo; Director of Photography: David Abel; Camera Operator: Joseph Biroc; Assistant Camera: Willard Barth and Clifford Stine; Additional Photography: Bill Williams; Special Effects: Vernon Walker; Art Direction: Van Nest Polglase and Carroll Clark; Set Dresser: Thomas Little; Costumes: Walter Plunkett; Gowns: Bernard Newman; Music Director: Max Steiner; Dance Director: William Hetzler; Ensembles Staged by: Hermes Pan; Sound: Hugh McDowell, Jr.; Music Recording: P.J. Faulkner Jr.; Technical Director: Peter Croft; Production Manager: C. J. White; Unit Manager: J. R. Crone; Script Clerk: Trudy Wellman; Research: Elizabeth McGaffey; Press Representative: S. Barrett McCormick; Electrician: James Vianna; Grip: Jim Davis; Propman: Thomas Little; Projectionist: Bill Hamberry; Still Photographer: Fred Hendrickson; Stand-in for Fred Astaire: Harry Cornbleth; Stand-in for Ginger Rogers: Marie Osborne; Stand-in for Helen Broderick: Helen Weber; Stand-in for Edward Everett Horton: Roy Horton. 101 minutes.

Songs (music and lyrics by Irving Berlin): "No Strings;" "Isn't This a Lovely Day (To Be Caught in the Rain);" "Top Hat;" "White Tie and Tails;" "Cheek to Cheek;" "The Piccolino."

Cast: Fred Astaire (Jerry Travers); Ginger Rogers (Dale Tremont); Edward Everett Horton (Horace Hardwick); Eric Blore (Bates); Eric Rhodes (Alberto Beddini); Helen Broderick (Madge Hardwick); Donald Meek (Curate); Florence Roberts (Curate's wife); Gino Corrado

(Lido Hotel Manager); Peter Hobbes (Call Boy); Lucille Ball (Flower Shop Clerk); Leonard Mudie (Flower Shop Proprietor); Robert Adair (Assistant Hotel Manager); Bud Flanagan (Passenger in Elevator); Ben Holmes, Nick Thompson, Tom Costello, John Impolite, Genaro Spagnoli, Ritz Rozelle, Phyllis Coghlan, Charles Hall, Anya Taranda, Henry Mowbray, Tom Ricketts, Tom Brandon, Roy Brent, Tito Blasco, Rosette Rosalie.

Video Availability: Turner Home Entertainment.

Assistant Editor

F6   STAGE DOOR (1937).

RKO-Radio. A Pandro S. Berman Production.

Director: Gregory La Cava. Editor: William Hamilton; Screenplay: Morrie Ryskind and Anthony Veiller; Based upon the 1936 play by Edna Ferber and George S. Kaufman; Director of Photography: Robert deGrasse; Art Director: Van Nest Polglase; Set Decorator: Darrell Silvera; Gowns: Muriel King; Wardrobe: Claire Cramer; Musical Director: roy Webb; Dance Director: Hermes Pan; Makeup: Mel Berns; Still Photography: John Miehle; Jewelry Design: Trabert and Hoeffer, Inc. Mauboussin; Sound: John L. Cass; Production Manager: J. R. Crone; Unit Manager: Fred A. Fleck; Research: Elizabeth McGaffey; Press Representative: S. Barrett McCormick; Stand-in for Katharine Hepburn: Pat Doyle; Stand-in for Ginger Rogers: Marie Osborne; Stand-in for Adolphe Menjou: Nick Borgeani; Stand-in for Gail Patrick: Grace Moody; Stand-in for Olive Hatch: Lucille Garon. 92 minutes.

Cast: Katharine Hepburn (Terry Randall [Sims]); Ginger Rogers (Jean Maitland); Adolphe Menjou (Anthony Powell); Gail Patrick (Linda Shaw); Constance Collier (Catherine Luther); Andrea Leeds (Kay Hamilton); Samuel S. Hinds (Henry Sims); Lucille Ball (Judith Canfield); Franklin Pangborn (Harcourt); William Corson (Bill); Pierre Watkin (Richard Carmichael); Grady Sutton (Butch); Frank Reicher (Stage Director); Jack Carson (Mr. Millbanks); Phyllis Kennedy (Hattie)l Eve Arden (Eve); Ann Miller (Annie); Margaret Early (Mary Lou); Jean Rouverol (Dizzy); Elizabeth Dunne (Mrs. Orcutt); Norma Drury (Olga Brent); Jane Rhodes (Ann Braddock); Peggy O'Donnell (Susan); Harriett Brandon (Madeline); Katherine Alexander, Ralph Forbes, Mary Forbes, Huntley Gordon (Cast of Stage Play); Theodore Kosloff (Dance

Director); Philip Morris (Announcer); Jack Richardson (Reporter); Harry Strang (Chauffeur); Julie Kingdon (Bernice Neimeyer); Frances Gifford (Mary McGuire); Lynn Gabriel (Tony); Mary Boward (Bobby); Jack Gargan and Gerda Mora (Dancing Instructors); Bob Perry (Baggage man); Josephine Whittell and Ada Leonard (Actresses); Linda Gray, Adele Pearce (Pamela Blake); Al Hill (Taxi Driver); Fred Santley (Dunkenfield); Jack Gardner (Script Clerk); Jack Rice (Playwright); Lynton Brent (Aide); Theodore Von Eltz (Elsworth); Ben Hendricks (Waiter); Larry Steers (Theatre Patron); Cynthia Westlake, Crawford Weaver, Frances Reid, Mary Jane Shower; Laurie Douglas, Marie Marks, Florence Reed, Max Wagner, Mary Louise Smith.

Awards: Academy Award nominations: Best Picture, Best Director, Best Screenplay, Best Supporting Actress (Leeds). National Board of Review Awards: 10 Best Films of the Year.

Video Availability: Turner Home Entertainment, Critics Choice Video, RKO Home Video.

F7 CAREFREE (1938).

RKO-Radio. A Pandro S. Berman Production.

Director: Mark Sandrich. Editor: William Hamilton. Sound Editor: T.K. Wood; Second Unit Director: Les Goodwins; Assistant Director: Argyle Nelson; Screenplay: Allan Scott and Ernest Pagano; Director of Photography: Robert de Grasse; Second Unit Photography: Bill Williams; Special Effects: Vernon Walker; Art Direction: Van Nest Polglase and Carroll Clark; Set Dresser: Darrell Silvera; Wardrobe: Edward Stevenson; Miss Rogers' Gowns: Howard Greer; Music Director: Victor Baravalle; Dance Director: Hermes Pan; Rehearsal Dance Directors: Bill Brande and Vasso Pan; Rehearsal Pianist: Hal Borne; Sound: Hugh McDowell, Jr.; Music Recording: P.J. Faulkner Jr.; Unit Manager: Fred Fleck; Makeup: Mel Berns; Still Photographer: John Miehle; Stand-in for Fred Astaire: Harry Cornbleth and Dorothy Panter; Stand-in for Ginger Rogers: Marie Osborne; Stand-in for Ralph Bellamy: Chuck Colean; Stand-in for Luella Gear: E. Cobb; Stand-in for Clarence Kolb: W. Stewart. 83 minutes.

Songs (words and music by Irving Berlin): "Since They Turned 'Loch Lomond' Into Swing;" "I Used to Be Color Blind;" "The Yam;" "Change Partners;" "The Night Is Filled With Music (instrumental background).

Cast: Fred Astaire (Tony Flagg); Ginger Rogers (Amanda Cooper); Ralph Bellamy (Stephen Arden); Luella Gear (Aunt Cora); Jack Carson (Connors); Clarence Kolb (Judge Travers); Franklin Pangborn (Roland Hunter); Walter Kingsford (Dr. Powers); Kay Sutton (Miss Adams); Robert B. Mitchell and his St. Brendan's Boys (Themselves); Hattie McDaniel (Hattie); Charles Coleman (Doorman); Richard Lane (Henry); Paul Guilfoyle (Elevator Operator); Tom Tully, Edward Gargan (Policemen); Jack Arnold (Radio Announcer); Frank Moran (Taxi Driver); James Burtis (Glass Truck Driver); Ted Manjean, Fred Sweeney (Men on bike path); Jane Woodworth, Marge Nelon, George DeNormand, Bobby Rose, Cliff Bergere, Dorothy Haas, L. Wood, Marek Wyndheim, Donald Kerr, H. Bailey, Phyllis Kennedy, Harold Minjir, B. Barbour, R. Ochman, Allan Scott, Jack Rice, Bert Morehouse, Bob Thatcher, Harry Campbell, Peggy Carroll, Jimmy Finlayson, Grace Hayle, Edward Gargan.

Video Availability: Turner Home Entertainment. RKO Home Video.

F8   HAVING WONDERFUL TIME (1938).

RKO-Radio.

Director: Alfred Santell (substantially re-shot by George Stevens); Screenplay: Arthur Kober; Additional Dialogue: Morrie Ryskind and Ernest Pagano; Based on the 1937 play by Arthur Kober; Director of Photography: Robert de Grasse; Special Effects: Vernon Walker; Art Direction: Van Nest Polglase; Assistant Art Director: Perry Ferguson; Assistant Director: James Anderson; Editor: William Hamilton; Set Dresser: Darrell Silvera; Gowns: Edward Stevenson and Renee; Music Director: Roy Webb; Sound: John E. Tribby; Research: Elizabeth McGaffey; Makeup: Mel Berns; Still Photography: John Miehle. 71 minutes.

Cast: Ginger Rogers (Teddy Shaw); Douglas Fairbanks, Jr. (Chick Kirkland); Peggy Conklin (Fay Coleman); Lucille Ball (Miriam); Lee Bowman (Maxwell "Buzzy" Pangwell); Eve Arden (Henrietta); Dorothea Kent (Maxine); Richard "Red" Skelton (Itchy); Donald Meek (P.U. Rogers); Jack Carson (Emil Beatty); Clarence M. Wilson (Mr. G.);

Allan Lane (Mac); Grady Sutton (Gus); Shimen Ruskin (Shrimpo); Dorothy Tree (Frances); Leona Roberts (Mrs. Shaw); Harlan Briggs (Mr. Shaw); Inez Courtney (Emma); Juanita Quigley (Mabel); Etienne Giardot (Mr. "G"); Margaret Seddon (Mrs. "G"); Kirk Windsor (Henry); Netty Jane Rhodes (Singer); George Meeker and Ronnie Rondell (Subway Mashers); Elise Cavanna (Office Supervisor); Mary Bovard, Frances Gifford, Peggy Montgomery, Baby Marie Osborne, Mary Jane Irving, Wesley Barry, Stanley Brown, Kay Sutton, Dorothy Day, Lynn Bailey, Tommy Watkins, Cynthia Hobard Fellows, Steve Putnam, William Corson, Bob Thatcher, Ben Carter, Russell Gleason, Florence Lake, Vera Gordon.

Video Availability: RKO Home Video.

F9   THE STORY OF VERNON AND IRENE CASTLE (1939).

RKO-Radio. A Pandro S. Berman Production.

Producer: George Haight; Director: H.C. Potter; Editor: William Hamilton. Sound Editor: T.K. Wood; Second Unit Director: Les Goodwins; Assistant Director: Argyle Nelson; Screenplay: Richard Sherman; Adaptation: Oscar Hammerstein II and Dorothy Yost; Based upon the book "My Husband" (1919) and the short story "My Memories of Vernon Castle" in Everybody's Magazine (November, 1918 - March 1919) by Irene Castle; Director of Photography: Robert de Grasse; Special Effects: Vernon Walker; Montage: Douglas Travers; Art Direction: Van Nest Polglase and Perry Ferguson; Set Dresser: Darrell Silvera; Wardrobe: Walter Plunkett; Music Director: Victor Baravalle; Dance Director: Hermes Pan; Sound: Richard Van Hessen; Technical Advice: Irene Castle; Stand-ins: Harry Cornbleth, Robert Strange, Ida Shoemaker, George Rogers, Evelyn Cobb and Dorothy Panter; 93 minutes.

Songs: "Only When You're In My Arms" by Con Conrad, Bert Kalmar and Harry Ruby; "Oh, You Beautiful Doll" by A. Seymour Brown and Nat D. Ayer; "Glow Little Glow Worm" by Lillia Cayley Robinson and Paul Lincke; "By The Beautiful Sea" by Harold Atteridge and Harry Carroll; "Row, Row, Row" by William Jerome and James V. Monaco; "The Yama Yama Man" by Collin Davis and Karl Hoschna; "Come Josephine In My Flying Machine" by Alfred Bryan and Fred Fisher; "By The Light of the Silvery Moon" by Edward Madden and Gus Edward; "Cuddle Up A Little Closer" by Otto Harbach and Karl Hoschna; "King

Chanticleer (Texas Tommy)" by Nat D. Ayer; "While They Were Dancing Around" by Joseph McCarthy and James V. Monaco; "The Darktown Strutters' Ball" by Shelton Brooks, French lyrics by Elsie Janis; "Rose Room" by Harry Williams and Art Hickman; "Tres Jolie Waltz" by Emil Waldteufel; "Syncopated Walk" by Irving Berlin; "Maxixe Dengozo" by Ernesto Nazareth; "Little Brown Jug" by Joseph W. Winner; "You're Here and I'm Here" by Harry B. Smith and Jerome Kern; "Chicago" by Fred Fisher; "Hello, Frisco, Hello" by Gene Buck and Louis A. Hirsch; "Way Down Yonder in New Orleans" by Henry Creamer and Turner Layton; "Take Me Back to New York Town" by Andrew B. Sterling and Harry von Tilzer; "It's a Long Way to Tipperary" by Jack Judge and Harry Williams; "Hello, Hello, Who's Your Lady Friend?" by Worton David and Bert Lee and Harry Fragson; "Destiny Waltz" by Sidney Baynes; "Nights of Gladness" Charles Ancliffe; "Missouri Waltz" by J. R. Shannon, Frederick Logan and John Eppell.

Cast: Fred Astaire (Vernon Castle); Ginger Rogers (Irene Castle); Edna Mae Oliver (Maggie Sutton); Walter Brennan (Walter); Lew Fields (Himself); Etienne Girardot (Papa Aubel); Janet Beecher (Mrs. Foote); Rolfe Sedan (Emile Aubel); Leonid Kinsky (Artist); Robert Strange (Dr. Foote); Douglas Watson (Student Pilot); Clarence Derwent (Papa Louis); Sonny Lamont (Charlie); Frances Mercer (Claire Ford); Victor Varconi (Grand Duke); Donald MacBride (Hotel Manager); Adrienne D'Ambricourt (Landlady); Jacques Lory (Cab Driver); Elspeth Dudgeon (Dowager); Milton Owen (Recruiting Officer); Bruce Mitchell, Jack Carson (Directors); Ethel Haworth (Young Girl); George Irving (General Brooke); Russell Hicks (Colonel); Peggy Carrol, Tiny Jones, Dorothy George, Ida May Johnson, Hal K. Dawson, Eleanor Hansen, Mary Brodell, Marjorie Bell, Kay Sutton, Fred Reinhold.

Notes: Robert Wise's last film as Assistant Editor was also Fred Astaire and Ginger Rogers' last film as an RKO team. Astaire and Rogers reunited a decade later at M-G-M for The Barkleys of Broadway. The real Vernon and Irene Castle appeared in a feature film in 1915: The Whirl of Life.

Video Availability: Turner Home Entertainment.

Editor

F10 BACHELOR MOTHER (1939).

   RKO-Radio.

   Produced by B. G. DeSylva: Executive Producer: Pandro S. Berman; Director: Garson Kanin; Editors: Henry Berman and ROBERT WISE. Screenplay: Norman Krasna; Story: Felix Jackson; Director of Photography: Robert de Grasse; Special Effects: Vernon Walker; Art Direction: Van Nest Polglase and Carroll Clark; Set Decoration: Darrell Silvera; Gowns: Irene; Musical Score: Roy Webb; Sound: Richard Van Hessen; Assistant Director: Edward Killy; Stand-ins: Dorothy Panter, Dick Crockett, Stuart Hall, Fred Fuller and R. Feldman. 82 minutes.

   Cast: Ginger Rogers (Polly Parish); David Niven (David Merlin); Charles Coburn (J.B. Merlin); Ernest Truex (Investigator); E.E. Clive (Butler); Elbert Coplen, Jr. (Johnnie); Frank Albertson (Freddie Miller); Ferike Boros (Mrs. Weiss); Leonard Penn (Jerome Weiss); Paul Stanton (Hargraves); Frank M. Thomas (Doctor); Edna Holland (Matron); Dennie Moore (Mary); June Wilkins (Louise King); Gerald Oliver-Smith (Hennessy); Leona Roberts (Old Lady); Hal K. Dawson (Judge); Barbara Pepper (Hostess); Hugh Prosser (Chauffeur); Renie Riano (Amy Mellish); Charles Halton (Doctor); Baby Garcia, Irving Bacon, Estelle Taylor, Peggy Carroll, Jane Woodworth, Ethel Haworth, Roger Hunt, Dan Clark, John Lang, Jean De Briac, Frank Corcasi, Fred Fuller, Dick Crockett, Ed Rochelle, Florence Lake, Chester Clute, R. Feldman, Dorothy Panter, Monte Vandergrift, John Laing, Dean Kaye.

   Notes: Working titles: Nobody's Wife and Little Mother. First filmed as Kleine Mutter in Hungary in 1935. Re-made as Bundle of Joy (1956).

   Wise Comments: "When I started cutting on my own I worked with Garson Kanin. I was assigned to go up on the set and stand by with him because he was from the stage and not too knowledgeable about film techniques. Kanin had been an actor and was very, very sensitive about the actor and his problems. It's always valuable for a director to have had experience as an actor. I didn't and I've very often regretted it." [A57]

Video Availability: Critics Choice Video, Facets Multimedia.

F11   FIFTH AVENUE GIRL (1939).

RKO-Radio. A Pandro S. Berman Production.

Produced and Directed by Gregory La Cava; Editors: Henry Berman and ROBERT WISE. Screenplay: Norman Krasna; Story: Felix Jackson; Director of Photography: Robert de Grasse; Special Effects: Vernon Walker; Art Direction: Van Nest Polglase and Perry Ferguson; Set Decoration: Darrell Silvera; Costumes: Howard Greer and Irene Greer; Musical Score: Roy Webb; Musical Score: Russell Bennett; Sound: John L. Cass; Assistant Director: Edward Killy; Stand-ins: Dorothy Panter, Skeets Noyes, Frank Kneedland and Sue Shannon. 82 minutes.

Cast: Ginger Rogers (Mary Gray); Walter Connolly (Alfred Borden); James Ellison (Mike); Tim Holt (Tim Borden); Verree Teasdale (Martha Borden); Kathryn Adams (Katherine Borden); Franklin Pangborn (Higgins); Ferike Boros (Olga); Louis Calhern (Dr. Kessler); Theodore von Eltz (Terwilliger); Alexander D'Arcy (Maitre d'hotel); Cornelius Keefe (Tommy Hopkins); Manda Lane (Amanda); Robert Emmett Keane (Seal Expert); Earl Richards (Skippy); Florence Lake (Slavey); Harold Langdon, Dick Hogan, (Boys); Peggy Stewart (Girl); Kathryn Hohn.

Video Availability: Turner Home Entertainment, RKO Home Video.

F12   THE HUNCHBACK OF NOTRE DAME (1939).

RKO-Radio.

Produced by Pandro S. Berman. Directed by William Dieterle. Edited by William Hamilton and ROBERT WISE. Music Composed and Adapted by Alfred Newman. Screenplay: Sonya Levien; Adaptation: Bruno Frank; Based upon the 1831 novel by Victor Hugo; Director of Photography: Joseph H. August; Special Effects: Vernon Walker; Art Direction: Van Nest Polglase and Al Herman; Set Decoration: Darrell Silvera; Costumes: Walter Plunkett; Sound: John E. Tribby; Assistant Directors: Argyle Nelson and Edward Killy; Technical Advisors: Louis Vandenecker and Rudi Feld; Makeup: Perc Westmore; Production Manager: J.R. Crone; Assistants to William Dieterle: Peter Berneis,

Erich Pommer Jr. and Michael Audley; Stand-ins: Gale Mogul, Raida Rae, Frank Mills, Sailor Vincent, Sue Shannon, Dick Crockett, Ray Atchley, Murray Darcy, Grace Moody, Edna Marisle, George Bax, Carda Rae, Hope Taylor, Ned Davenport, Jack Paul and Bill Brennan. 117 minutes.

Cast: Charles Laughton (Quasimodo); Maureen O'Hara (Esmeralda); Sir Cedric Hardwicke (Frollo); Thomas Mitchell (Clopin); Edmond O'Brien (Gringoire); Alan Marshal (Phoebus); Walter Hampden (Archbishop); Harry Davenport (King Louis XI); Katharine Alexander (Fleur's Mother); George Zucco (Procurator); Fritz Leiber (Old Nobelman); Etienne Girardot (Doctor); Helene Whitney (Fleur); Minna Gombell (Queen of Beggars); Arthur Hohl (Olivier); George Tobias (Beggar); Rod La Rocque (Phillipo); Spencer Charters (Court Clerk); Kathryn Adams and Diane Hunter (Fleur's Companions); Siegfried Arno (Tailor); Peter Godfrey (Priest); John Fowler (Nobleman); Hector Sarno (Knight); Joe Mack (Workman in Play); Harry Vejar (Noble); Dewey Robinson (Butcher); Ferdinand Munier (Defense Attorney); Gretl Sherk (Lissy); Edward Groag (Moon); Vallejo Gantner (Merchant); Thom Fox (Jupiter); Louis Adlon (Venus); Charles Hall (Mercury); Robert Schiller (Saturn); Otto Hoffman (Judge); Lionel Belmore (Clergy in Play); Rudolph Steinbeck (Peasant in Play); Ray Long (Dancer of Death); Arthur DeLac (Mars); Tempe Pigott (Madalaine); Dick Dickinson (Wooden-leg Man); Alan Spear (Contortionist); Ward Shattuck and Earl Clyde (Jugglers); Harold DeGarro (Stiltwalker); Louis Valaris (Tightrope Man); Antonio Pina (Ladder Man); Consuela Melandez and Eddie Abdul (Singers); Vangie Beilby and Elsie Prescott (Contestants); Gisela Wernesik (Grandmother); Al Herman (Short Fat Soldier); Angela Molinos [Clarke] (Helene); Victor Kilian (Old Hangman); Arthur Millet (Count Graville); Raymond Hatton and Russ Powell (Ugly Men); James Fawcett (Roll-ball Man); Barlowe Borland (Dubois); Paul Newlan (Whipper); Margaret McWade (Younger Sister); Margaret Seddon (Older Sister); Lillian Nicholson (Delys' Servant); Ione Reed and Marie Bodie (Doubles for Maureen O'Hara); Archie Butler (Double for Alan Marshall); Jack Perrin and George De Normand (Doubles for Rod La Rocque); Eddie Dew, Charles Drake, Harry Fleischman, Fred Mellinger, Louis Jean Heydt, Gail Patrick, Laura Hope Crews, Rube Schaffer, Peter Godfrey, Victor Metzetti, Billy Jones, Frank Mills, Walter O. Stahl, Cecil Weston, John Laird, Richard Clayton, Lew King, Bud Fine, Nestor Paiva, Ted Lorch, Harry Weil, Alexander Granach, George Souzanne, Gene Clark, John Lawrence, George Barrows, Mary Lou Wentz, Laurie Hale, Louis Williams, Eleanor Pellapreau.

Notes: An earlier version of <u>The Hunchback of Notre Dame</u> was produced in 1923 starring Lon Chaney. It was re-made in 1957 starring Anthony Quinn and Gina Lollabrigida and in 1982 (for television; video title: <u>Hunchback</u>) starring Anthony Hopkins and Lesley-Ann Down.

Video Availability: RKO Home Video, VidAmerica Inc.

F13   <u>MY FAVORITE WIFE</u> (1940).

RKO-Radio. A Leo McCarey Production.

Produced by Leo McCarey. Directed by Garson Kanin. Screenplay: Bella and Samuel Spewack; Story: Bella Spewack, Samuel Spewack and Leo McCarey; Additional Writing: John McClain and Bert Granet; Director of Photography: Rudolph Mate; Art Director: Van Nest Polglase; Associate Art Director: Mark-Lee Kirk; Set Decoration: Darrell Silvera; Editor: ROBERT WISE; Assistant Editor: Mark Robson. Music: Roy Webb; Gowns: Howard Greer; Sound: John E. Tribby. 93 minutes.

Cast: Cary Grant (Nick Arden); Irene Dunne (Ellen Arden); Gail Patrick (Bianca Bates); Randolph Scott (Stephen Burkett); Ann Shoemaker (Ma Arden); Scotty Beckett (Tim Arden); Mary Lou Harrington (Chinch Arden); Donald MacBride (Hotel Clerk); Hugh O'Connell (Johnson); Pedro De Cordoba (De Kohlmar); Brandon Tynan (Dr. Manning); Leon Belasco (Bartender); Earl Hodgins (Clerk of Court); Clive Morgan and Bert Moorhouse (Lawyers); Florence Dudley and Jean Acker (Witnesses); Cy Ring (Contestant); Joe Cabrillas (Phillip); Frank Marlowe (Photographer); Thelma Joel (Miss Rosenthal); Horace MacMahon (Truck Driver); Chester Clute (Shoe Salesman); Eli Schmudkler (Janitor); Franco Corsaro (Waiter); Pat West (Caretaker); Cy Kendall (Detective); Ronnie Rondell and Matty Roubert (Bell Boys); Roque Guinart (Waiter); Edward Emerson, Bruce MacFarlane and Joe Bernard (Reporters); Bill Cartledge (Page Boy); Sue Moore (Maid); Edna Holland, Victor Kilian, Ellen Lowe, Peggy Martin and Frank Ellis.

Notes: Based very loosely on Alfred, Lord Tennyson's poem <u>Enoch Arden</u>. The story was to be remade in 1962 as <u>Something's Got To Give</u> but all footage was shelved when star Marilyn Monroe died. It was eventually remade by 20th Century-Fox as <u>Move Over Darling</u> (1963) starring James Garner and Doris Day. Garson Kanin took over direction of <u>My Favorite Wife</u> after Leo McCarey was involved in a near-fatal automobile accident.

Video Availability: Turner Home Entertainment.

F14   DANCE, GIRL, DANCE (1940).

RKO-Radio.

Executive Producer: Harry E. Edington; Producer: Erich Pommer; Director: Dorothy Arzner; Screenplay: Tess Slesinger and Frank Davis; Director of Photography: Russell Metty (some sources list Joseph August as cinematographer); Special Visual Effects: Vernon Walker; Edited by ROBERT WISE; Assistant Director: James H. Anderson; Art Direction: Van Nest Polglase; Associate Art Director: Al Herman; Set Decoration: Darrell Silvera; Gowns: Edward Stevenson; Musical Direction: Edward Ward and Ernst Matray; Sound: Hugh McDowell Jr. 90 minutes.

Songs: "Oh Mother, What Do I Do Now?" and "Morning Star" by Bob Wright and Chet Forrest; "The Jitterbug Bit" by Wright, Forrest and Ed Ward; "Urban Ballet" by Ward.

Cast: Maureen O'Hara (Judy O'Brien); Lucille Ball (Bubbles/Tiger Lily); Louis Hayward (Jimmy Harris); Virginia Field (Elinor Harris); Maria Ouspenskaya (Madame Basilova); Ralph Bellamy (Steve Adams); Mary Carlisle (Sally); Katharine Alexander (Miss Olmstead); Edward Brophy (Dwarfie); Walter Abel (Judge); Harold Huber (Hoboken Gent); Ernest Truex (Bailey No. 1); Chester Clute (Bailey No. 2); Lorraine Krueger (Dolly); Lola Jensen (Daisy); Emma Dunn (Mrs. Simpson); Vivian Fay (The Ballerina); Sidney Blackmer (Puss in Boots); Ludwig Stossel (Caesar); Erno Verebes.

Notes: Working title: Have It Your Own Way. Arzner took over direction of this film after Roy Del Ruth quit due to "creative differences" with producer Pommer.

Wise Comments: "I don't think Dorothy stepped into a very enviable position because it was a weak project with a weak script. She improved the work in the film very much. It certainly was not a great film by any means, but it never could have been because of the weaknesses that were inherent in the project. She worked well on it." [A85]

Video Availability: Turner Home Entertainment, RKO Home Video.

F15   CITIZEN KANE (1941).

RKO-Radio. A Mercury Production.

Executive Producer: George J. Schaefer; Produced by Orson Welles and John Houseman. Directed by Orson Welles. Screenplay: Orson Welles and Herman J. Mankiewicz; Photographed by Gregg Toland; Music: Bernard Herrmann: Editor: Mark Robson and ROBERT WISE; Art Direction: Van Nest Polglase, Hilyard Brown and Perry Ferguson; Set Decoration: Darrell Silvera; Set Dresser: Al Fields; Gowns: Edward Stevenson; Makeup: Maurice Seiderman; Special Effects: Vernon L. Walker; Sound: Bailey Fesler and James G. Stewart; Assistant Director: Richard Wilson. 119 minutes.

Cast: Orson Welles (Charles Foster Kane); Joseph Cotten (Jedediah Leland); Everett Sloane (Mr. Bernstein); Dorothy Comingore (Susan Alexander Kane); Agnes Moorehead (Mrs. Kane); Ray Collins (Boss James W. Gettys); William Alland (Thompson and Newsreel Narrator); Paul Stewart (Raymond); Ruth Warrick (Emily Norton Kane); George Coulouris (Walter Parks Thatcher); Erskine Sanford (Herbert Carter); Richard Barr (Hillman); Fortunio Bonanova (Matisti); Joan Blair (Georgia); Buddy Swann (Kane at 8); Harry Shannon (Kane Sr.); Sonny Bupp (Kane III); Gus Schilling (The Headwaiter); Alan Ladd (Reporter); Philip Van Zandt (Mr. Rawlston); Al Eben (Mike); Charles Bennett (Entertainer); Milt Kibbee (Reporter); Edith Evanson (Nurse); Tom Curran (Teddy Roosevelt); Irving Mitchell (Dr. Corey); Georgia Backus (Miss Anderson); Arthur Kay (Conductor); Tudor Williams (Chorus Master); Herbert Corthell (City Editor) Benny Rubin (Smather); Edmund Cobb (Reporter); Frances Neal (Ethel); Robert Dudley (Photographer); Ellen Lowe (Miss Townsend); Gino Carrado (Gino the Waiter); Louise Currie, Eddie Coke, Walter Sande, Arthur O'Connell (Reporters).

Awards: Academy Awards: Best Original Screenplay. Academy Awards Nominations: Best Picture, Best Actor (Welles), Best Black and White Cinematography, Best Editing (Wise), Best Interior Decoration, Best Sound, Best Original Score. New York Film Critics: Best Picture. National Board of Review: 10 Best Films of the Year.

Video Availability: The Voyager Company (Criterion Collection; laser disc), RKO Home Video (cassette). The Criterion disc "Citizen Kane: 50th Anniversary Edition" includes the original theatrical trailer, Welles' early, experimental film Hearts of Age, The Legacy of 'Citizen Kane', a tribute to Welles featuring interviews with 35 directors and cinematographers, and <u>The Making of a Film Classic</u> by Robert Carringer, which contains photographs, storyboards and sketches.

F16   <u>ALL THAT MONEY CAN BUY</u> (1941)

RKO-Radio. A William Dieterle Production.

Produced and Directed by William Dieterle. Associate Producer: Charles L. Glett; Screenplay: Stephen Vincent Benet and Dan Totheroh; Based upon Benet's short story "The Devil and Daniel Webster"; Editor: ROBERT WISE; Music: Bernard Herrmann; Art Director: Van Nest Polglase; Set Decorator: Darrell Silvera; Costumes: Edward Stevenson; Assistant Director: Argyle Nelson; Photography: Joseph August; Special Effects: Vernon L. Walker; Sound: Hugh McDowell Jr. and James G. Stewart;. Running Time: See <u>Notes</u> below.

Cast: Walter Huston (The Devil); Edward Arnold (Daniel Webster); Simone Simon (Belle); James Craig (Jabez Stone); Jane Darwell (Ma Stone); Gene Lockhart (Squire Slossum); John Qualen (Miser Stevens); H.B. Warner; Anne Shirley (Mary Simpson Stone); Frank Conlan; Lindy Wade (Young Daniel); Jeff Corey (Tom Sharp); George Cleveland.

Notes: The working title of the film was <u>A Certain Mr. Scratch</u>. RKO considered several titles, including <u>Black Daniel</u>, <u>It Can Happen To You</u>, <u>The Devil To Pay</u> and <u>Temptation</u>.

The film was previewed at 109 minutes on July 16, 1941 under the title <u>Here Is A Man</u>. When it opened on October 16, 1941, three minutes had been cut and the title changed to <u>All That Money Can Buy</u>. Some prints over the next few years were titled <u>The Devil and Daniel Webster</u>. In 1952, the film was cut again, to 84 minutes, and the title changed to <u>Daniel and the Devil</u>. It was in this short form that the film existed for almost four decades.

According to Bruce Eder's liner notes of The Criterion Collection laser disc, a 106 minute 16mm print was discovered in 1990. Although worn, the print was cleaned, transferred digitally and retimed. The best surviving 35mm elements were combined with the scenes which existed only in 16mm and the result was issued on laser disc in 1991 by The Voyager Company.

Video Availability: The Voyager Company (Criterion Collection; laser disc), Columbia TriStar Home Video, Sultan Entertainment. The Criterion disc contains a supplemental audio commentary by film historian Bruce Eder and, discussing Bernard Herrmann's musical score, Steve Smith.

F17   THE MAGNIFICENT AMBERSONS (1942).

RKO-Radio/A Mercury Production.

Direction and Screenplay by Orson Welles (and, uncredited, ROBERT WISE); Photography: Stanley Cortez (and, uncredited, Harry J. Wild and Russell Metty); Editor: ROBERT WISE (and, uncredited, Mark Robson); Music: Bernard Herrmann (and, uncredited, Roy Webb); Art Direction: Mark-Lee Kirk; Gowns: Edward Stevenson; Special Effects: Vernon L. Walker; Sound Recording by Bailey Fesler and James G. Stewart; Production Manager: Freddie Fleck. 88 minutes [see Notes]

Cast: Tim Holt (George Minafer); Anne Baxter (Lucy); Joseph Cotten (Eugene Morgan); Agnes Moorehead (Fanny); Ray Collins Jack); Erskine Sanford (Benson); Dolores Costello (Isabel); Richard Bennett (Major Amberson); Don Dillaway (Wilbur Minafer); J. Louis Johnson (Sam); Charles Phipps (Uncle John); Georgia Backus, Gus Schilling.

Notes: A silent version of Tarkington's novel was filmed in 1925. It was called Pampered Youth and starred Cullen Landis and Alice Calhoun.

After completing production on The Magnificent Ambersons, Orson Welles went to South America to film It's All True as part of the Pan American good will effort. RKO had promised to send Wise there so that Welles could supervise the final editing. The two met at The Fleischer animation studios in Miami and worked for three days editing the film and recording Welles' narration. Because of the Second World War the government placed an embargo on international civilian travel, which kept Wise from then following Welles back to South America. Welles attempted to supervise the editing by telephone and cable; Wise once received a thirty-five page cable with editorial instructions. When this laborious process was completed, The Magnificent Ambersons was about two and a half hours long.

After a disastrous sneak preview in Pomona, California in

March, 1942, during which the audience laughed at the film and talked back to the characters on the screen, RKO head George J. Schaefer ordered Wise to cut The Magnificent Ambersons by some forty minutes. "My assessment of it has always been that the audiences were in a completely different frame of mind now that the war was on," Wise said. "Everybody was keyed up and impatient and they just didn't have the patience for this artistic piece of work." While this shorter cut seemed to satisfy audiences a little more, some still complained about the downbeat ending. A more positive ending with stars Joseph Cotten and Agnes Moorehead was filmed by production manager Freddie Fleck.

Wise, making his uncredited directing debut, shot a few new bridging scenes, including the one in which George Minafer (Tim Holt) brings a letter to his mother (Dolores Costello) and the moody fireside soliloquy by the dying Major Amberson (Richard Bennett).

Wise Comments: "It was too bad that [Welles] could not get back up to work on the film with us but it was one of those impasse situations and nothing could be done about it. I think, though, that the film keeps its unity. There have been statements made that Orson thought his film was ruined by the studio and by us, but I say that is wrong; we can't have ruined it because it has come down through the years as a classic in its own right. I would be the first to admit that as a work of art it was a much better film in its original form, no question about it." [A85]

Awards: Academy Award nominations: Best Picture, Best Black and White Cinematography, Best Interior Decoration, Best Supporting Actress (Moorehead). New York Film Critics: Best Actress (Moorehead).

Video Availability: The Voyager Company (The Criterion Collection; laser disc), RKO Home Video, VidAmerica Inc. The Criterion Collection disc contains the entire shooting script, complete storyboards for all scenes, Orson Welles' Mercury Theatre radio production of The Magnificent Ambersons, footage from Pampered Youth, an interview with Welles and a supplementary audio track by film historian Robert Carringer which details the history of the production and describes the scenes which were eventually cut from the film.

F18   SEVEN DAYS' LEAVE (1942).

RKO-Radio.

Produced and Directed by Tim Whelan; Screenplay: William
Bowers, Ralph Spence, Curtis Kenyon and Kenneth Earl; Director of
Photography: Robert de Grasse; Editor: ROBERT WISE; Special Effects:
Vernon L. Walker; Art Direction: Albert D'Agostino and Carroll Clark;
Set Decoration: Darrell Silvera and Michael Ohrenbach; Gowns: Renie;
Recorded by Robert Guhl; Assistant Director: Sam Rumann;
Choreography: Charles Walters; Music Director: C. Bakaleinikoff; Vocal
and Musical Advisor: Ken Darby; Songs: Lyrics by Frank Loesser, Music
by James McHugh; Associate Producer: George Arthur. 87 minutes.

Cast: Lucille Ball (Terry); Victor Mature (Johnny Good); Ginny
Simms (Herself); Peter Lind Hayes (Mickey); Arnold Stang (Bitsy);
Walter Reed (Ralph Bell); Wallace Ford (Sergeant Mead); Buddy Clark
(Clarky); King Kennedy (Gifford); Charles Andre (Chedgie); Harry
Holman (Justice of Peace); Addison Richards (Major Collins); Ralph
Edwards (Himself); Harold Peary (Gildersleeve); Freddy Martin and his
Orchestra; Les Brown and his Orchestra; Lynn, Royce and Vanya;
Edward and Co.; Sergio Orta (Himself); Jack Gardner (Announcer);
Willie Fung (Houseboy); Ronnie Rondell (Miller - Chauffeur); Richard
Martin, Frank Martinelli, Russell Hoyt (Financial Trio); Henry DeSoto
(Matre d'Hotel); Charles Hall, Ed Thomas (Waiters); Mary Halsey, Julie
Warren, Mary Stuart, Ariel Heath (Bits); Doug Evans, Bob LeMond
(Announcers); Ralph Dunn (Cop); John Morris (Attendant); Allen Wood
(Groom); Eric Wilton (Bill's Butler); Charles Flynn (Guard); Max Wagner
(Military Police).

Notes: Tradeshown in Los Angeles October 12, 1942.

Video Availability: Turner Home Entertainment.

F19   BOMBARDIER (1943).

RKO-Radio.

Produced by Robert Fellows; Directed by Richard Wallace;
Editor: ROBERT WISE; Screenplay: John Twist; Story: John Twist and
Martin Rackin; Music: Roy Webb; Musical Director: C. Bakaleinikoff;

"Song of the Bombardiers" music by M.K. Jerome and lyrics by Jack Scholl; Director of Photography: Nicholas Musuraca; Special Effects: Vernon L. Walker; Art Directors: Albert D'Agostino and Al Herman; Set Decorations: Darrell Silvera and Claude Carpenter; Gowns: Renie; Recorded by Bailey Fesler; Re-recorded by James G. Stewart; Montage: Douglas Travers; Assistant Director: Edward Killy. 99 minutes.

Cast: Pat O'Brien (Major Chick Davis); Randolph Scott (Capt. Buck Oliver); Anne Shirley (Burt Hughes); Eddie Albert (Tom Hughes); Robert Ryan (Joe Connor); Walter Reed (Jim Carter); Barton MacLane (Sergeant Dixon); Leonard Strong (Jap Officer); Richard Martin (Chito Rafferty); Russell Wade (Paul Harris); James Newill (Captain Rand); John Miljan (Chaplain Craig); Charles Russell (Instructor); Bruce Edwards (Lt. Ellis); Harold Landon (Pete Jordon); Margie Stewart (Mamie); Joe King (General Barnes); Abner Biberman (Jap Sergeant); Russell Hoyt (Photographer); Wayne McCoy (Instructor); Bud Geary (Sergeant); Warren Mace, George Ford (Co-Pilots); Charles Flynn (Radio Operator); Erford Gage (Meyer); Charles D. Brown (Col. Converse); Neil Hamilton (Colonel); Herbert Heyes (General); Robert Middlemass, Lee Shumway, Ed Peil (Officers); Lloyd Ingraham (Colonel); Paul Parry (Capt. Driscoll); James Craven (Major Morris); Cy Ring (Capt. Rendall); John Barclay (Bit); John Calvert (Illusionist); Paul Fix (Big Guy); Murray Alper (Little Boy); Mike Lally (Co-Pilot); Joey Ray (Navigator); Kirby Grant, Eddie Dow (Pilots); John James (Lieutenant); Stan Andrews, John Sheehan, Walter Fenner, Bert Moorhouse (Congressman); Hugh Beaumont (Bit Soldier); Marty Faust (Bit); Allen Wood (Army Clerk); Larry Wheat (Doctor Bit); Dick Winslow (Navigator).

Notes: Tradeshown in Los Angeles May 10, 1943.

Video Availability: Turner Home Entertainment, RKO Home Video.

F20   THE FALLEN SPARROW (1943).

RKO-Radio.

Produced by Robert Fellows; Directed by Richard Wallace (and, uncredited, ROBERT WISE); Editor: ROBERT WISE; Screenplay: Warren Duff; Based upon a novel by Dorothy B. Hughes; Director of Photography: Nicholas Musuraca; Special Effects: Vernon L. Walker; Art Directors: Albert D'Agostino and Mark-Lee Kirk; Production

Designer: Van Nest Polglase; Assistant Director: Sam Rumann; Music:
Roy Webb; Musical Director: C. Bakaleinikoff. 93 minutes.

Cast: John Garfield (Kit); Maureen O'Hara (Toni Dunne); Walter
Slezak (Dr. Skaas); Patricia Morison (Barby Taviton); Martha O'Driscoll
(Whitney Hamilton); John Banner (Anton); Hugh Beaumont (Otto
Skaas); Sam Goldenberg (Prince deNamur); John Miljan (Inspector
Tobin); Russell Wade (Ab Hamilton); George Lloyd (Sergeant Moore);
Russ Powell (Priest); James Farley (Bartender); Lee Phelps (Cop);
Charles Lung (Carlo); Rosina Galli (Mama); Marte Faust (Chef - Carlo's
Cafe); Lillian West (Receptionist); Miles Mander (Dr. Gudmundson);
Edith Evanson (Murse); Bud Geary (Cab Caller); William Edmunds
(Papa); Stella Le Saint (Bit Woman in Street); Nestor Paiva (Jake); Jack
Carr (Danny); Jane Woodworth, Patti Brill, Margie Stewart, Margaret
Landry, Mary Halsey (Bits); Andre Charlot (Peter); Eric Wilton (Butler);
Erford Gage (Roman); Joe King (Desk Sergeant); Rita Gould (Det); Taxi
Driver (Mike Lally); Foly Franquelli (Gypsy Dancer); Al Rhein (Bit Man);
Edgar Sherrod (Butler); Billy Mitchell (Porter); Babe Green, George
Sherwood (G-Men).

Notes: Tradeshown in Los Angeles August 17, 1943.

Video Availability: Image Entertainment (laser disc).

F21 THE IRON MAJOR (1943).

RKO-Radio.

Produced by Robert Fellows; Directed by Ray Enright; Editors:
ROBERT WISE and Philip Martin, Jr.; Screenplay: Aben Kandel and
Warren Duff; Original Story: Florence E. Cavanaugh; Director of
Photography: Robert de Grasse; Art Direction: Albert D'Agostino and
Carroll Clark; Set Decoration: Darrell Silvera and Al Fields; Costumes:
Edward Stevenson; Technical Direction: William P. "Hiker" Joy and
Ernest E. La Branche; Music: Roy Webb; Music Director: C.
Bakaleinikoff. 85 minutes.

Cast: Pat O'Brien (Frank Cavanaugh); Ruth Warrick (Florence);
Leon Ames (Robert Stewart); Robert Ryan (Father Donovan); Russell
Wade (Manning); Bruce Edwards (Lieutenant Jones); Richard Martin
(Davie); Bob Thom, Arnold Stanford (Bit Soldiers); Lew Harvey (Bit
Lieutenant); Robert Anderson, Mike Lally, Barbara Hale (Bits); Bud

Geary (Bit Sergeant); Walter Brooke (Lieutenant Stone); Louis Jean Heydt (Recruiting Sergeant); Mary Currier (Nurse); Frank Puglia (French Major); Pierre Watkin (Major White); Walter Fenner (Doctor); Louis Borell (French Officers); Billy Roy (Bob as a boy); Robert Winkler (Frank as a boy); Henry Rocquemore (Evans); Joel Davis, Teddy Infuhr (Bit Boys); Bert Moorhouse, Cy Ring, Wilbur Mack (Bit Men); Wheaton Chambers (Army Doctor); Myron Healey (Paul); Dean Benton (William); Kirk Alyn (John); James Jordon (Philip); Victor Kilian, Jr. (Francis); Margaret Landry (Sis Cavanaugh); Ian Wolfe (Professor Runnymead); Harry Tyler, Eddie Woods (Friends); Pat O'Malley (Charlie); Elena Duran, Ramon Ros (Dancers).

Video Availability: Turner Home Entertainment.

Director

F22   THE CURSE OF THE CAT PEOPLE (1944)

RKO-Radio.

Produced by Val Lewton; DIRECTED BY Gunther von Fritsch and ROBERT WISE; Assistant Director: Harry D'Arcy; Script: DeWitt Bodeen; Photography: Nicolas Musuraca; Editor: J.R. Whittredge; Art Direction: Albert S. D'Agostino and Walter E. Keller; Set Decorators: Darrell Silvera and William Stevens; Music: Roy Webb; Music Director: C. Bakaleinikoff; Songs: "Ruben Ranzo", "It Came Upon a Midnight Clear", "Shepherds Shake Off Your Drowsy Sleep." Costumes: Edward Stevenson; Sound Recordist: Francis M. Sarver; Sound Re-recordist: James G. Stewart. 70 minutes.

Cast: Simone Simon (Irena Dubrovna Reed); Kent Smith (Oliver Reed), Jane Randolph (Alice Reed); Ann Carter (Amy); Elizabeth Russell (Barbara); Julia Dean (Julia Farren); Eve March (Miss Calahan); Erford Gage (Captain of Guard); Sir Lancelot (Edward); Joel Davis (Donald); Juanita Alvarez (Lois); Charley Bates (Jack); Gloria Donovan, Ginny Wren and Linda Ann Bieber (Little Girls); Sarah Selby (Miss Plummett); Mel Sternlight (State Trooper); Lord Buckley (bit).

Notes: Filmed in RKO Studios, Hollywood, August 25 - October 4, 1943. U.S. premiere: March, 1944. G. B. premiere: October, 1944.

Reviews: "Masquerading as a routine case of Grade B horrors --and it does very well at that job -- the picture is in fact a brave, sensitive, and admirable little psychological melodrama..." (James Agee, The Nation, April 1, 1944)

"A marvelous little film...one of the least condescending and least sentimental forays ever made into what James Agee called 'the poetry and danger of childhood.'" (Phil Hardy; B38)

Wise Comments: "The director [Gunther von Fritsch] whose first feature it was, was going very slow in terms of his shooting. These were, after all, very low-budget films with short, twenty day schedules. This chap had shot his whole schedule and only covered half the script. Lewton and Sid Rogell, head of the [RKO] B-picture unit, were unable to goose him up and make him go faster. Now they were going to take him off and they wanted me to take over the directing on Monday. I had been asking them...for a chance to direct, so I was thrilled, but also very concerned because I had been working with the director as an editor. I had to go back and work with him that night, and I had a reluctance to take over under those circumstances. I was told by RKO that he was not going to be on the set Monday morning and some other man would be there directing. Now, it could be me or somebody else but it wasn't going to be the original director. So under those circumstances I had no choice but to accept. That's why the split credit appears on the screen." [A85]

"I had cut two or three films for Richard Wallace [Fallen Sparrow and Bombardier]; he happened to be shooting on the same lot when I took over Curse of the Cat People....he came...on the set to wish me well and he said, "Bobbie, I have only one piece of advice to give you; one, but it's very important. It's simply this: if the scene seems a little slow on the set it'll be twice as slow in the projection room." It's proved to be so true. Very seldom in putting a film together do you wish you had played it a little slower on the set; more often than not you wish that you had picked it up a little bit, that the tempo was a little faster." [A57]

Video Availability: Turner Home Entertainment.

F23 <u>MADEMOISELLE FIFI</u> (1944).

RKO-Radio

Produced by Val Lewton; DIRECTED BY ROBERT WISE; Asst. Director: Sam Ruman; Script: Josef Mischel, Peter Ruric. Based on "Boule de Suif" and "Mademoiselle Fifi" by Guy de Maupassant. Photography: Harry Wild; Editor: J.R. Whittredge; Art Direction: Albert S. D'Agostino, Walter E. Keller; Set Decorators: Darrell Silvera, Al Fields; Special Effects: Vernon L. Walker; Music: Werner Heymann; Musical Director: C. Bakaleinikoff; Songs: "Three Captains," "Drinking Song;" Costumes: Edward Stevenson; Sound Recordist: Francis M. Sarver; Sound Re-recordist: James G. Stewart. 69 minutes.

Cast: Simone Simon (Elizabeth Rousset); John Emery (Jean Cornudet); Kurt Kreuger (Lt. von Eyrick "Fifi"); Alan Napier (Count De Breville); Helen Freeman (Countess De Breville); Jason Robards, Sr. (Wholesaler in Wines); Norma Varden (Wholesaler's Wife); Romaine Callender (Manufacturer); Fay Helm (Manufacturer's Wife); Edmund Glover (Young Priest); Charles Waldron (Cure' of Cleresville); Mayo Newhall (M. Follenvie); Lillian Bronson (Mme. Follenvie); Alan Ward (Coach Driver); Daun Kennedy (The Maid); William Von Wymetal (The Major); Max Willenz (The Captain); Marc Cramer (The Lieutenant); John Good (Fritz); Allan Lee (Hostler); Frank Mayo (Sgt. at Inn); Margaret Landry (Eva); Rosemary La Planche (Amanda Blondini); Marie Lund (Helene); Margie Stewart (Pamela); Violet Wilson (Aunt Marie); Tom Burton and Steven Winston (Ulhans); Paul Marion (Devoir); Ed Allen (Soldier); Richard Drumm (German Sentry); Victor Cutler (Soldier Waiter).

Notes: Filmed at RKO Studios in Hollywood March 23 - April 22, 1944. U.S. premiere: August, 1944. John Ford's <u>Stagecoach</u> (1939) was also loosely based upon de Maupassant's story "Boule de Suif."

Reviews: "There is a gallant, fervent quality about the whole picture, faults and all, which gives it a peculiar kind of life and likableness, and which signifies that there is one group of men working in Hollywood who have neither lost nor taken care to conceal the purity of their hope and intention." (James Agee, <u>The Nation</u>, December 2, 1944).

Video Availability: Facets Multimedia.

F24   THE BODY SNATCHER (1945).

RKO-Radio

Produced by Val Lewton; DIRECTED BY ROBERT WISE; Executive Producer: Jack J. Gross; Assistant Director: Harry Scott; Script: Philip MacDonald, Carlos Keith (pseudonym for Val Lewton). Based on the story by Robert Louis Stevenson. Director of Photography: Robert De Grasse; Editor: J.R. Whittredge; Art Direction: Albert S. D'Agostino, Walter E. Keller; Set Decorators: Darrell Silvera, John Sturtevant; Music: Roy Webb; Musical Director: C. Bakaleinikoff; Costumes: Renie; Sound Recordist: Bailey Fesler; Sound Re-recordist: Terry Kellum. RCA Sound System. 78 minutes.

Songs: "We'd Better Bide a Wee," "Spit Song," "When Ye Gang Awa," "Jamie," "Will Ye No Come Back Again," "Bonnie Dundee."

Cast: Boris Karloff (John Gray); Bela Lugosi (Joseph); Henry Daniell (Dr. "Toddy" MacFarlane); Edith Atwater (Meg Camden MacFarlane); Russell Wade (Donald Fettes); Rita Corday (Mrs. Marsh); Sharyn Moffett (Georgina Marsh); Donna Lee (Street Singer); Robert Clarke (Richardson); Carl Kent (Gilchrist); Jack Welch (Boy); Larry Wheat (Salesman); Mary Gordon (Mrs. Mary McBride); Jim Moran (Angus, Horse Trader); Aina Constant (Maid); Bill Williams (Student); Sammy Blum (Waiter).

Reviews: "...a little dull and bookish; but it explodes into a...poetic, horror climax - which, however, is sustained for only the last few minutes." (James Agee, The Nation, September 29, 1945)

"...the last passage...is as all-out, hair-raising a climax to a horror film as you are ever likely to see." (Time September, 1945)

"Superbly controlled and strikingly literate. Wise's direction is...a model of discretion and assurance, making excellent use of de Grasse's chiaroscruo lighting." (Phil Hardy; B38)

Notes: Filmed at RKO Studios in Hollywood, October 25 - November 17, 1944. Exteriors shot on the Hunchback of Notre Dame set at the RKO ranch in the San Fernando Valley. Interiors filmed on Sound Stage 4 at RKO Studios. A set constructed for Jacques Tourneur's Experiment Perilous (1944) was used for MacFarlane's anatomy room. Released March, 1945. New York premiere: May, 1945. G.B. premiere: December, 1945.

The Body Snatcher is based loosely on the exploits of early 19th Century grave robbers Burke and Hare, although they are not themselves characters in the film. These grotesques are portrayed in The Flesh and The Fiends (a.k.a. Mania, directed by John Gilling, 1960), Burke and Hare (directed by Vernon Sewell, 1971), and The Doctor and The Devils (directed by Freddie Francis, 1985).

Wise Comments: "Boris Karloff was very excited about the [opportunity] to do The Body Snatcher because he saw in this role the chance to prove himself as an actor, not just somebody who was marvelous in horror pictures of the monster type. He was a highly educated and sensitive and well-read man with great taste. Lugosi was another story. He actually was rather forced into the piece; somebody in the front office thought it would be marvelous exploitation to have Karloff and Lugosi in the same movie. He had been ill for some time and his English wasn't terribly good. I had no major problems with him; it was just hard to get through to him. I almost had to nurse him through the scenes whereas Karloff was very up and very stimulated by the prospect of what he could do with the character of Gray, the grave robber." [A85]

"Val Lewton was such a tremendously interesting and creative man. He was really a creative producer, who contributed so much to his films without ever imposing on the director. So much of the texture, look and feel of Val's films came from him. His credo was, 'The greatest fear that people have is fear of the unknown.' That's what intrigued me about doing The Haunting later: you hear some things and don't really see anything. I can't tell you how many people said it was the scariest movie they'd ever seen, and it all came from Val and my days with him." (Interview with Frank Thompson, September, 1990).

Video Availability: Turner Home Entertainment, RKO Home Entertainment.

F25 A GAME OF DEATH (1945).

RKO-Radio

Produced by Herman Schlom. DIRECTED BY ROBERT WISE. Screenplay: Norman Houston. Based on the story "The Most Dangerous Game" by Richard Connell. Director of Photography: J. Roy Hunt; Art Direction: Albert S. D'Agostino and Lucius Croxton; Set Decoration: Darrell Silvera and James Altwes; Sound: Phillip Mitchell and James G. Stewart; Editor: J. R. Whittredge; Special Effects: Vernon L. Walker; Music: Paul Sawtell; Musical Director: C. Bakaleinekoff; Assistant Director: Doran Cox. 72 minutes.

Cast: John Loder (Rainsford); Audrey Long (Ellen Trowbridge); Edgar Barrier (Eric Kreiger); Russell Wade (Robert Trowbridge); Russell Hicks (Whitney); Jason Robards (Captain); Gene Stutenroth (Pleshke); Noble Johnson (Carib); Robert Clarke (Helmsman); Edmund Glover (Quartermaster); Bruce Edwards (Collins); Jimmy Jordan (Steward); Vic Romito (Mongol); Jimmy Dimo (Bulgar).

Notes: Filmed previously as The Most Dangerous Game (released in Great Britain as The Hounds of Zaroff) in 1932. Stock footage from Most Dangerous Game was used. Remade as Run For The Sun (1956) and as Hard Target (1993).

Reviews: The Film Daily called A Game of Death "absorbing, weird and exciting." (November 28, 1945)

Wise Comments: "A Game of Death was...a film that I really didn't want to make. I don't like remakes and I had a problem trying to put any sizable creativity into the film. I was compelled to use stock shots of the Great Danes running through the swamps from the original picture and as I would go into a given sequence I would have flash in front of me the scene as it was shot originally. I found this terribly hard to overcome. Since I was not enthusiastic about the whole project, it was just a question of giving it everything I could." [A85]

F26   CRIMINAL COURT (1946).

RKO-Radio

Executive Producer: Sid Rogell. Produced by Martin Mooney. DIRECTED BY ROBERT WISE. Screenplay: Lawrence Kimble; Story: Earl Felton; Director of Photography: Frank Redman, A.S.C.; Art Direction: Albert S. D'Agostino and Lucius O. Croxton; Editor: Robert Swink; Music: Paul Sawtell. Musical Director: C. Bakaleinikoff. 63 minutes.

Songs: "Couldn't Sleep a Wink Last Night" and "A Lovely Way to Spend an Evening" (Harold Adamson and Jimmy McHugh). "Comin' 'Round the Mountain."

Cast: Tom Conway (Steve Barnes); Martha O'Driscoll (Georgia Gale); June Clayworth (Joan Mason); Robert Armstrong (Vic Wright); Addison Richards (Gordon, the D.A.); Pat Gleason (Joe West); Steve Brodie (Frankie Wright); Robert Warwick (Marquette); Phil Warren (Bill Brannegan); Joe Devlin (Clark J. Brown "Brownie"); Lee Bonnell (Gil Lambert); Robert Clarke (Charlie, Dance Director); Nancy Saunders (Secretary); Tom Noonan (Cab Driver); Phil Dunham (Councilman Hankinson); Dick Rush (Wilson); Sam Ash (Jennings); Colin Kenny (Roberts); Homer Dickenson (Butler); Robert Smith (Officer Doyle); Johnny Indrisano (Headwaiter); Tony Barrett (Reporter); Lee Frederick (Kellogg); Harry Harvey (Judge Bennett); Jason Robards (Al Marah); Mike Lally (Reporter); Carl Hansen (Reporter); Charles Regan (Asst. District Attorney); Max Rose (Jim, the Bailiff); Joe Gray (1st Gunman); Jack Gordon (2nd Gunman); Eddie Borden (Court Clerk); Stanley Blystone (Sam, the Bartender); Don Kerr (Page boy); Sam Flint (Inspector Carson); Joe Bernard (Luther, the Valet); Alf Haugan (Foreman of the Jury).

Reviews: The Motion Picture Herald called Criminal Court "an entertaining melodrama" with an "exciting plot." (August 10, 1946.

Wise Comments: "Just one of those B pictures that one does under stock contract. I didn't like the story at all but if you don't do things, turn them down, they put you on suspension - you can't work any place else. I was most anxious to make more films and learn more, so as a consequence I made several films at the period that I was not keen about rather than just sit it out on suspension." [A57]

Video Availability: RKO Home Video.

F27   BORN TO KILL (1947).

RKO-Radio

Executive Producer: Sid Rogell. Produced by Herman Schlom. DIRECTED BY ROBERT WISE. Screenplay: Eve Greene and Richard Macaulay. From the novel "Deadlier Than The Male" by James Gunn. Director of Photography: Robert de Grasse, A.S.C.; Art Direction: Albert S. D'Agostino and Walter E. Keller; Editor: Les Millbrook; Music:

Paul Sawtell. 92 minutes.

Cast: Lawrence Tierney (Sam Wild); Claire Trevor (Helen Trent); Walter Slezak (Arnett); Phillip Terry (Fred Grover); Audrey Long (Georgia Staples); Elisha Cook, Jr. (Marty); Isabel Jewell (Laury Palmer); Esther Howard (Mrs. Kraft); Kathryn Card (Grace); Tony Barrett (Danny); Grandon Rhodes (Inspector Wilson); Sam Lufkin, Sayre Dearing, Sammy Shack, Joe Dixon (Crap dealers); Ruth Brennan (Sally); Tom Noonan (Bell Boy); Al Murphy (Cab Driver); Phil Warren (Chauffeur); Ben Frommer (Delivery boy); Netta Packer (Mrs. Perth); Lee Frederick (Desk Clerk); Demetrius Alexis (Maitre d'); Beatrice Maude (Cook); Ellen Corby (Maid); Martha Hyer (Maid); Jean Fenwick (Margaret Macy); Reverend Neal Dodd (Bit Clergyman); Napoleon Whiting (Porter); Perc Launders (Detective Bryson); Stanley Stone (Train Conductor); Jason Robards (Conductor); Scott Brady (Conductor).

Note: Working title: Deadlier Than the Male. Title in Great Britain: Lady of Deceit.

Reviews: According to Variety (April 16, 1947), the film "packs a wallop in individual scenes, but [its] plot frequently is too complicated for its own good. Robert Wise in his direction generated a menacing note which seldom lets down."

Virginia Wright of The Los Angeles Daily News (July 3, 1947) said that Born to Kill "is a sordid, exaggerated affair, unredeemed by any sharpness of characterization or tightness of story line."

Video Availability: Turner Home Entertainment.

F28   MYSTERY IN MEXICO (1948).

RKO-Radio

Produced by Sid Rogell. DIRECTED BY ROBERT WISE. Associate Producer: Joseph Noriega; Screenplay: Lawrence Kimble; Story: Muriel Roy Bolton; Director of Photography: Jack Draper; Art Director: Gunther Gerzso; Editor: Samuel E. Beetley; Music: Paul Sawtell; Musical Director: C. Bakaleinikoff. Songs by Johnny Burke and Jimmy Van Heusen. 66 minutes.

Songs: "Something in Common," "At The Psychological Moment," "I Could Get Along Without You," "Rolling in Rainbows."

Cast: William Lundigan (Steve); Jacqueline White (Victoria); Ricardo Cortez (Norcross); Tony Barrett (Carlos); Jacqueline Dalya (Dolores); Walter Reed (Glenn); Jose Torvay (Swigart); Jaime Jimenez (Pancho); Antonio Frausto (Pancho's father); Dolores Camerillo (Pancho's mother); Eduardo Casado (Commandant Rodriquez); Thalia Draper (Floracita); Carlos Musquiz (Luis Otero); Armando Silvestre (Benny); Freddie Romero (Jose); Alfonso Jimenez (Lopez, the Driver); Conchita Gentil Arcos (Benny's Mother); Lilia Plancarte (Benny's Sister); Suzi Crandall (Airline Hostess); Marilyn Mercer (Airline Hostess); William Forrest (Powers).

Reviews: "...sufficient pace to hold casual attention. There's a sticky romantic pursuit and a flip treatment of characters but good menace has been supplied as a balance by Robert Wise's direction." (Variety, June 23, 1948).

Notes: Filmed at Churubusco Studios in Mexico City. Released August 21, 1948. In the four years since Wise began directing, the cost of B movies had risen dramatically, from about $150,000 to about $200,000. RKO Executive Sid Rogell believed that A pictures could be made with B budgets in Mexico and sent Wise as (in his words) "a kind of guinea pig to go down there and try it. I think we found out that it wasn't necessarily so: the costs were not that much cheaper [nor] the results much better."

F29   BLOOD ON THE MOON (1948)

RKO-Radio

Produced by Sid Rogell and Theron Warth; DIRECTED BY ROBERT WISE; Screenplay: Lillie Hayward; Based on the Novel "Gunman's Choice" by Luke Short; Adaptation: Harold Shumate and Luke Short; Director of Photography: Nicolas Musuraca; Music: Roy Webb; Music Director: C. Bakaleinikoff; Art Direction: Albert S. D'Agostino and Walter E. Keller; Editor: Samuel E. Beetley. 88 minutes.

Cast: Robert Mitchum (Jim Garry); Barbara Bel Geddes (Amy Lufton); Robert Preston (Tate Riling); Walter Brennan (Kris Barden); Phyllis Thaxter (Carol Lufton); Frank Faylen (Jake Pindalest); Tom Tully

(John Lufton); Charles McGraw (Milo Sweet);   Clifton Young (Joe
Shotten); Tom Tyler (Frank Reardan); George Cooper (Fritz Barden);
Richard Powers [Tom Keene] (Ted Elser); Bud Osborne (Cap Willis); Zon
Murray (Nels Titterton); Robert Bray (Bart Daniels); Al Ferguson (Chet
Avery); Ben Corbett (Mitch Moten); Joe Devlin (Barney); Erville
Alderson (Settlmeir, liveryman); Robert Malcolm (Sheriff Manker);
Chris-Pin Martin (Bartender); Ruth Brennan (Townswoman); Harry
Carey, Jr. (Cowboy); Hal Taliaferro (Cowboy); Al Murphy (Cowboy);
Iron Eyes Cody (Toma).

Reviews: "...thoroughly satisfactory...well-acted, directed and
photographed...it was an honest touch to have Mitchum spend at least
three minutes screen time to regain his breath after a fight with
Preston." (Los Angeles Daily News, January 1, 1949).

"...shadow-filled, taut Western. Wise's direction and the locales
(mostly indoors) give the material a strong psychological dimension."
(Phil Hardy; B40)

Wise Comments: "It was my desire to try for the first time
maybe, at least in my memory, to show a real bar fight between a
couple of cowboys, and not the hoopla, bar-crashing, fellas over the
bar, everything in the mirrors, bottles all over the place, tables crashing
into the wall - to show an almost life and death struggle between the
two men who, as they fight, do get weary, do get out of breath...and
are scarcely able to stand when the fight is over. I tried very hard to
get that kind of realistic feeling in that fight." [A85]

Video Availability: Turner Home Entertainment.

F30   THE SET-UP (1949).

RKO-Radio

Produced by Richard Goldstone. DIRECTED BY ROBERT WISE.
Screenplay: Art Cohn (from the 1929 narrative poem by Joseph
Moncure March); Director of Photography: Milton Krasner; Art
Direction: Albert S. D'Agostino and Jack Okey; Set Decoration: Darrell
Silvera and James Altwies; Makeup: Gordon Bau, Joe Norrin and Bill
Phillips; Hairstyles: Hazel Rogers and Gale Roe McGarry; Assistant
Director: Edward Killy; Storyboards: Maurice Zuberano; Fight
Sequences staged by John Indrisano; Editor: Roland Gross; Music

Director: C. Bakaleinikoff; Sound: Phil Brigandi and Clem Portman;
Script Supervisor: Dan Ullmann. 72 minutes.

Cast: Robert Ryan (Bill "Stoker" Thompson); Audrey Totter
(Julie Thompson); George Tobias (Tiny); Alan Baxter (Little Boy);
Wallace Ford (Gus); Percy Helton (Red); Hal Fieberling (Tiger Nelson);
Darryl Hickman (Shanley); Kenny O'Morrison (Moore); James Edwards
(Luther Hawkins); David Clarke ("Gunboat" Johnson); Phillip Pine
(Souza); Edwin Max (Danny); Dave Fresco (Mickey); William B. Green
(Doctor); Abe Dinovitch (Ring Caller); Jack Chase (Hawkins' Second);
Mike Lally, Arthur Sullivan, William McCarter, Gene Delmont (Handlers);
Herbert Anderson (1st Husband); Jack Raymond (2nd Husband); Walter
Ridge (Manager); Helen Brown (1st Wife); Constance Worth (2nd
Wife); Jess Kirkpatrick (Older Gambler); Paul Dubov (Young Gambler);
Frank Richards (Bat); Jack Stoney (Nelson's Second); Archie Leonard
(Blind Man); John Butler (Blind Man's Companion); Larry Anzalone
(Mexican Fighter); Vincent Graeff (Newsboy); Bernard Gorcey (Tobacco
Man); Tom Noonan (Masher); Charles Wagenheim (Hamburger Man);
Billy Snyder (Barker); W. J. O'Brien (Pitchman); Frank Mills
(Photographer); Everett Smith (Tattoo Man); Ruth Brennan, Herman
Bodel, Ralph Volkie, Tony Merrill, Lillian Castle, Carl Sklover, Sam
Shack, Frances Mack, Andy Carillo, Charles Sullivan, Gay Waters,
Maxine Johnston, Dan Foster, Al Rhein (Bits); Bobby Henshaw
(Announcer); Dwight Martin (Glutton); Noble "Kid" Chissel (Handler);
Ben Moselle (Referee); Arthur Weegee Fellig (Timekeeper); Brian O'Hara
(Man With Cigar); Lynn Millan (Bunny); Donald Kerr (Vendor).

Notes: Filmed in 19 days (completed on November 11, 1949)
at the RKO Pathe Studio in Culver City, the Pacific Electrical Tunnel on
Temple Street in Los Angeles and at Ocean Park Arena. The 72 minute
running time represents the "real time" in which the story takes place.
Released March 29, 1949.

The Set-Up was produced during that chaotic period at RKO as
studio head Dore Schary was replaced by Howard Hughes. Wise had
only one more film to do under his current contract and, sensing that
Hughes' arrival would throw the studio into an uproar, was anxious to
move on. Hughes gave the film the green light, Wise completed it as
quickly as possible and, after one independent production at Warner
Bros., moved on to a new contract at 20th Century-Fox.

Reviews: "The Set-Up...is a rhetorical Robert Wise film,
overstating the malice in ordinary people (repeated near close-ups of a

blind fight fan yelling, 'go for his eyes'), but often good in the intermediate nonbrutal scenes in a penny arcade and a cheap hotel room." (Manny Farber, 1949).

Awards: Robert Ryan, Best Actor, 1949 Cannes Film Festival. The film received the Critics' Choice award at the same Festival.

Video Availability: Critics Choice Video.

F31   THREE SECRETS (1950).

Warner Bros.

Produced by Milton Sperling. DIRECTED BY ROBERT WISE. Screenplay: Martin Rackin and Gina Kaus; Director of Photography: Sid Hickox; Art Director: Charles H. Clarke; Editor: Thomas Reilly; Original Music: David Buttolph. Charles K. Feldman Group Productions. A United States Pictures Production. 98 minutes.

Cast: Eleanor Parker (Susan Chase); Patricia Neal (Phyllis Horn); Ruth Roman (Ann Lawrence); Frank Lovejoy (Bob Duffy); Leif Erickson (Bill Chase); Ted de Corsia (Del Prince); Edmon Ryan (Hardin); Larry Keating (Mark Harrison); Katherine Warren (Mrs. Connors); Arthur Franz (Paul Radin); Duncan Richardson (Johnny); Peter Brocco (Stephani); Frank Fenton (Macdonald); Joel Allen (Operator); Oil Warren (Assistant); Paul Picerni (Sgt.); Glenn Denning (Pilot); Mike Mahoney (G. I.); Russ Conway (Captain); William Self (Sgt.); Jay Adler (City Editor); Frances Williams (Delia); Nana Bryant (Supervisor); Janet Warren (Asst. Supervisor); Margaret Bert (Maid); Bill Welsh (Radio Commentator); John Morgan (Ralph); Mary Alan Hokanson (Betty); Cherie May (Nurse); Edna Holland (Receptionist); Ray Hyke (Trooper); Ralph Montgomery (Vendor); George Lynn (Reporter); Billy Bevan (Jackson); Mervin Williams, Rory Mallinson, Ross Elliott (Reporters); John Butler (Bartender); Cathy Dart (Switchboard Operator); Tim Graham (Reporter); David McMahon (Man); Willard Waterman (Man); Mack Williams (Army Doctor); Christian Drake (Radio Technician); Wheaton Chambers (Man with Dog); Edmond Glover (Ranger); Charles Wagenheim (2nd Man); Perc Launders (Chauffeur); Lester Dorr (Houseman); Weldon Boyle (Room Clerk); William Tennen (Bobby Lynch); John Dehner (Gordon Crosley); Eleanor Audley (Warden); Eula Guy (Matron); Frank Wilcox (Reporter); Kenneth Tobey (Officer).

Reviews: "For director Robert Wise the assignment is conspicuously successful. Actually he has three stories to tell in one, and they are all frankly melodramatic. His finesse in weaving them together and in highlighting three intriguing performances by a trio of feminine stars is the element that endows 'Three Secrets' with much of its punch." [Hollywood Reporter August 29, 1950]

"An arresting, original story...potent dramatic entertainment. It is adult fare with particularly strong appeal for women. Dialogue has maturity and is delivered with glib realism." [Film Daily August 30, 1950]

Notes: Released October 14, 1950. Working title: The Rock Bottom. After his contract with RKO ended, Wise made this one feature for Warner Bros. An unpretentious little soap opera, concerning three women who each gave up a child for adoption five years earlier who learn that one of their sons is the sole survivor of an air crash, Three Secrets is surprisingly effective. Wise himself remains fond of the flashback sequence starring Patricia Neal and Frank Lovejoy. "It was one of three films I made with Patricia Neal," he said. "Marvelous lady!" [A59]

Video Availability: Republic Home Video.

F32   TWO FLAGS WEST (1950).

20th Century-Fox.

Produced by Casey Robinson. DIRECTED BY ROBERT WISE. Screenplay: Casey Robinson; Story: Frank S. Nugent and Curtis Kenyon; Director of Photography: Leon Shamroy; Art Director: Lyle Wheeler and Chester Gore; Set Decoration: Thomas Little, Fred J. Rode; Editor: Louis Loeffler; Music: Hugo Friedhofer; Musical Direction: Alfred Newman; Orchestration: Earle Hagen and Maurice DePackh; Makeup Artist: Ben Nye; Special Photographic Effects: Fred Sersen; Wardrobe Direction: Charles Le Maire; Costume Designer: Edward Stevenson; Sound: Alfred Bruzlin and Harry M. Leonard. 92 minutes.

Cast: Joseph Cotten (Col. Clay Tucker); Linda Darnell (Elena Kenniston); Jeff Chandler (Kenniston); Cornel Wilde (Capt. Mark Bradford); Dale Robertson (Lem); Jay C. Flippen (Sgt. Terrance Duffy); Noah Beery Jr. (Cy Davis); Harry Von Zell (Ephriam Strong); John

Sands (Lt. Adams); Arthur Hunnicutt (Sgt. Pickens); Jack Lee (Courier); Harry Carter (Lt. Reynolds); Ferris Taylor (Dr. Magowan); Sally Corner (Mrs. Magowan); Everett Glass (Rev. Simpkins); Marjorie Bennett (Mrs. Simpkins); Roy Gordon (Capt. Stanley); Lee MacGregor (Cal); Aurora Castillo (Maria); Stanley Andrews (Col. Hoffman); Don Garner (Ash Cooper); Robert Adler (Hank).

Reviews: "...an interesting premise for solid action and fast pace...more emphasis on the...characters...than in shoot-'em-up drama. Robert Wise's direction manages to build a not inconsiderable air of expectancy in moving towards the fighting climax." (Variety, October 11, 1950).

"...spectacular, suspenseful, convincing, lightning-paced drama. Virtually every member of [the cast] delivers a sterling performance under the expert direction of Robert Wise." (Box Office, October 14, 1950).

Notes: Tradeshown at 20th Century-Fox Studio in Westwood, California on October 6, 1950. Working title: Trumpet to the Morn.

F33   THE HOUSE ON TELEGRAPH HILL (1951).

20th Century-Fox.

Produced by Robert Bassler. DIRECTED BY ROBERT WISE. Screenplay: Elick Moll and Frank Partos. From the novel "The Frightened Child" by Dana Lyon. Director of Photography: Lucien Ballard A.S.C.; Art Direction: Lyle Wheeler and John De Cuir; Set Decorations: Thomas Little and Paul S. Fox; Wardrobe: Charles LeMaire; Costumes: Renie; Editor: Nick De Maggio; Musical Director: Alfred Newman; Music: Sol Kaplan. Orchestration: edward Powell and Maurice de Packh; Makeup: Ben Nye; Special Photographic Effects: Fred Sersen; Sound: George Leverett and Harry M. Leonard. 93 minutes.

Cast: Richard Basehart (Alan Spender); Valentina Cortesa (Victoria Kowelska); William Lundigan (Major Marc Bennett); Fay Baker (Margaret); Gordon Gebert (Chris Dunakova); Kei Thing Chung (James C. Callahan); John Burton (Mr. Whitmore); Katherine Neskill (Mrs. Whitmore); Mario Siletti (Tony, grocer); Charles Wagenheim (Man at Accident); David Clarke (Mechanic); Tamara Schee (Maria); Natasha

Lytess (Karin Dunakova); Ashmead Scott (Inspector Harvery); Marl Young (Chinese Girl Singer); Tom McDonough (Farrell, cop); Henry Rowland (Staff Sgt./Interpreter); Les O'Pace (UNRA Sgt.); Don Kohler (Fowler, chemist); Harry Carter (Detective Ellis); Dot Farley (Saleswoman).

Notes: Filmed on location in San Francisco. Released June, 1951.

F34   THE DAY THE EARTH STOOD STILL (1951).

20th Century-Fox.

Produced by Julian Blaustein. DIRECTED BY ROBERT WISE. Screenplay: Edmund H. North. From the story "Farewell to the Master" by Harry Bates. Music: Bernard Herrmann; Director of Photography: Leo Tover; Art Direction: Lyle Wheeler and Addison Hehr; Set Decoration: Thomas Little, Claude Carpenter; Editor: William Reynolds, A.C.E.; Wardrobe: Charles Le Maire; Klaatu's Costume Designed by Perkins Bailey; Costumes: Travilla; Makeup: Ben Nye; Special Photographic Effects: Fred Sersen; Sound: Arthur H. Kirback, Harry M. Leonard; Technical Advisor: Dr. Samuel Herrick. 92 minutes.

Cast: Michael Rennie (Klaatu); Patricia Neal (Helen Benson); Hugh Marlowe (Tom Stevens); Sam Jaffe (Dr. Barnhardt); Billy Gray (Bobby Benson); Frances Bavier (Mrs. Barley); Lock Martin (Gort); Drew Pearson (Himself); Frank Conroy (Harley); Carleton Young (Colonel); Fay Roope (Major General); Edith Evanson (Mrs. Crockett); Robert Osterloh (Major White); Tyler McVey (Brady); James Seay (Government Man); John Brown (George Barley); Marjorie Crossland (Hilda); Glenn Hardy (Interviewer); Kim Spalding, Larry Dobkin (Medical Corps Captains); Howard Negley (Colonel); Bill Gentry, Kip Whitman, Michael Capanne, Michael Mahoney (Sentries); James Doyle (Medical Corps Major); Michael Ragan (Army Captain); Jack Daly, Herman Stevens (Bits); Marshall Bradford (Government Man); John M. Reed (Tank Driver); Ted Pearson (Colonel); John Close (Captain); David McMahon (English Sgt.); Sammy Ogg, Ricky Regan (Bit Boys); Gayle Pace (Captain); Grady Galloway (American Radar Operator); John Costello (Cockney); Eric Corrie, Michael Ferr (British Soldiers); Hassas Khayyam (Indian Announcer); House Peters, Jr. (M.P. Captain); Rush Williams (M.P. Sergeant); Olan Soule (Mr. Kurll); Gil Herman (Government Man); James Craven (Business Man); Herbert Lytton (Brigadier General);

Freeman Lusk (General Cutler); George Lynn (Colonel Ryder); John Burton (British Radio Announcer); Harry Harvey, Sr. (Taxi Driver); Harry Lauter (Platoon Leader); Charles Evans (Major General); Harlan Warde (Mr. Carlson); Wheaton Chambers (Jeweler); Elizabeth Flournoy (Evelyn, Jewelry Clerk); Dorothy Neumann (Secretary); Gabriel Heater, H.V. Kaltenborn, Elmer Davis (Commentators); Snub Pollard (Cabby); Major Sam Harris (Delegate);.

Notes: Filming began on April 9, 1951 and was completed on May 18. Klaatu's space ship stood 25 feet high and measured 350 feet in circumference and was built at a cost of $100,000, according to studio press materials. This full-size version had no back, so that craftsmen could stand behind it to operate the ship's exit ramp and the rotation of the saucer's hull. The ship was designed by Set Designer Lyle Wheeler and Addison Hehr. Because the script called for the ship's door to be perfectly concealed until opened, it was sealed over with plastic and coated with silver paint after every take. Additionally, a two-foot model and a seven-foot model of the ship were constructed for special effects scenes. Whenever the ship is seen in full view, it is one of these two models.

The company filmed for 42 days on the Fox back lot in Century City and, beginning on March 19, 1951, shot two weeks of second unit footage in Washington D.C. The second unit was directed by Bert Leeds.

Lock Martin, who played the robot Gort, was seven feet, seven inches tall and was employed as a doorman at Graumann's Chinese Theatre. His helmet was made of metal but the robot suit was made of foam rubber which was painted silver. The heat and claustrophobia of the suit were very hard on Martin. Bob Burns, a friend of Martin's, said [A74], "[Martin] loved the Gort part but it was really tiring for him. That last scene in the film nearly killed him. The script called for him to stand perfectly still on the ramp of the spaceship and with delays and retakes he spent almost five hours up there. He began to shake and in the film if you look hard enough you can see his hands fidgeting. Between the heat and the order to stand perfectly still, and the danger of falling, it was one of his most terrifying moments."

A clip was used in The Coneheads (1993). Working title: Journey to the World.

Awards: Golden Globe Award: Best Film Promoting International

Understanding.

Wise Comments: "I think you go about making science fiction believable to an audience by believing in it yourself. I think that's why The Day The Earth Stood Still was as believable to people as it was. We believed in it. We told it very directly, without a lot of phoniness; we tried to make it very realistic." [A85]

Video Availability: CBS/Fox Home Video, Facets Multimedia, Mike LeBell's Video.

F35   THE CAPTIVE CITY (1952).

   Aspen/United Artists.

   Produced by Theron Warth. DIRECTED BY ROBERT WISE. Screenplay: Alvin M. Josephy, Jr. and Karl Kamb; Story: Alvin M. Josephy, Jr.; Director of Photography: Lee Garmes; Editor: Ralph Swink; Music: Jerome Moross; Prologue/Epilogue: Senator Estes Kefauver; Sound: James G. Stewart; Musical Direction: Emil Newman; Production Design: Maurice Zuberano; Assistant Director: Ivan Volkman. 91 minutes.

   Cast: John Forsythe (Jim Austin); Joan Camden (Marge Austin); Harold J. Kennedy (Don Carey); Marjorie Crossland (Mrs. Sirak); Victor Sutherland (Murray Sirak); Ray Teal (Chief Gillette); Martin Milner (Phil Harding); Geraldine Hall (Mrs. Nelson); Hal K. Dawson (Clyde Nelson); Ian Wolfe (Rev. Nash); Gladys Hurlbut (Linda Percy); Jess Kirkpatrick (Anderson); Paul Newlan (Krug); Frances Morris (Mrs. Harding); Charles Wagenheim (Phone Man); Paul Brinegar (Police Sgt.); Vic Romito (Fabretti); Charles Regan (Gangster); Senator Estes Kefauver (Himself); Patricia Goldwater, Robert Gorrell, Glenn Judd, William C. Miller (Bits).

   Notes: Filmed on location in Reno, Nevada. Aspen Pictures was an independent production company founded by Wise and Mark Robson. The Captive City and Return to Paradise (1953, directed by Robson) were the only two pictures produced by Aspen. "...we made the entire thing in Reno," Wise said [A59]. "We used the newspaper there, the city hall, the streets. There was no process - we hung cameras on cars - we didn't shoot a foot in the studio. We shot it in 22 or 23 days. That was the first one I ever did entirely on location [until

Two People (1973)]. I've been on location many times, of course, but always based in a studio." Filming was completed in February, 1952 and the film was released on March 26, 1952.

According to a The New York Times article of March 30, 1952, Captive City was filmed with a new depth of focus lens developed by photographic technician Ralph Hoge. "With the standard lens used for long shots, it is not possible to maintain perfect focus and true definition of persons and objects in the foreground and the background. For this reason directors have to cut up the action in both close-up and long shots and in using the wide angle lens for distance it is necessary to put on the lights. The Hoge lens, says Mr. Wise, reduces the lighting requirements by 50 per cent (which means money saved) and also enables the director to shoot scenes in continuous action."

Reviews: "Unusual in its category [the film is] technically and atmospherically correct and is built around a story entirely believable in its every detail." (Box Office, April 5, 1952).

"Director-producer Wise builds each facet lucidly and pertinently as the cancerous undergrowth, festering in out-of-state Mafia killings, is unfolded. It's an exciting movie with only a few dull spots." (Los Angeles Daily News, May 17, 1952).

F36   SOMETHING FOR THE BIRDS (1952).

20th Century-Fox.

Produced by Samuel G. Engel. DIRECTED BY ROBERT WISE. Screenplay: I.A.L. Diamond and Boris Ingster; Based on Stories by: Boris Ingster, Alvin M. Josephy, Jr. and Joseph Petracca; Director of Photography: Joseph LaShelle, A.S.C.; Art Direction: Lyle Wheeler and George Patrick; Set Decoration: Thomas Little and Bruce Macdonald; Editor: Hugh S. Fowler; Wardrobe: Charles Le Maire; Costumes Designed by: Elois Jenssen; Music: Sol Kaplan; Musical Direction: Lionel Newman; Orchestration: Bernard Mayers; Special Photographic Effects: Ray Kellogg; Sound: Arthur L. Kirbach and Harry M. Leonard; Assistant Director: Henry Weinberger. 81 minutes.

Cast: Victor Mature (Steve Bennett); Patricia Neal (Anne Richards); Edmund Gwenn (Johnnie Adams); Larry Keating (Patterson); Gladys Hurlbut (Mrs. Rice); Hugh Sanders (Grady); Christian Rub (Leo);

Wilton Graff (Taylor); Walter Baldwin (Bigelow); Archer MacDonald (Lemmer); Richard Garrick (Chandler); Ian Wolfe (Foster); Russell Gaige (Winthrop); Louise Lorimer (Mrs. Winthrop); John Brown (Mr. Lund); Camillo Guercio (Duncan); Joan Miller (Mac); Madge Blake (Mrs. Chadwick); Norman Field (Judge); Sam McDaniel (Server); Gordon Nelson (O'Malley); Emmett Vogan (Beecham); John Ayres (Congressman Walker); Charles Watts (Jessup); Rodney Bell (Announcer); Norma Varden (Congresswoman Bates); Leo Curley (Congressman Macy); John Maxwell (Congressman Craig); Elizabeth Flournoy (Receptionist); Charlie Garrett (Secretary); Adele Longmire (Wave Lt. J. G.); Herbert Lytton (Captain); Morgan Brown (Waiter); Gene Foley, Dolly Jarvis (Secretaries); Tom McDonough (1st Deliveryman); David McMahon (2nd Deliveryman); Fred Datig Jr. (Bellhop); Richard Shackleton (Apprentice); Harry Hines, Bob Milton (Bellhops); John Hedloe (Young Man); Paul Power (Court Clerk); Abe Dinovitch, Larry Arnold, Olga Borget, Holger Bendixen, Angela De Witt, Curt Furberg, Andrew Roud, Greta Ullman (Foreigners); Marshall Bradford (Admiral); Ralph Gamble (Butler); Robert Livingston (General); Ken Christy (1st V.I.P.); James Craven (2nd V.I.P.); Ralph Montgomery (Young Man); Roy Engel (Congressman Farrow); John Diggs (Counsel); Major Philip Kieffer (U.S. Marshall); Michael McHale, Edmund Cobb, John Alban, Tom Gibson, Ted Jordan (Reporters); Charles Conrad (Clerk); Mary Alan Hokansen (Receptionist); Dayton Lummis (Speaker); Maude Prickett (Woman with vacuum cleaner); Joan Shawlee (Woman in station); John Butler (Customer); Vince Townsend (Doorman); Charles Wagenheim (Cab Driver); Major Sam Harris, General Sam Savitsky (Guests); Jeffrey Sayre (Technician).

Reviews: "...a warm, mirthful comedy, rich in satire that lands several devastating swipes at the Washington scene. The package is neatly handled by Robert Wise, whose deft direction highlights the comedy to a hilarious degree while driving over the more serious intent underlying the film." (Hollywood Reporter, October 1, 1952).

F37 DESTINATION GOBI (1953).

20th Century-Fox.

Produced by Stanley Rubin. DIRECTED BY ROBERT WISE. Screenplay: Everett Freeman; Based on the Story "Ninety Saddles for Kengtu" By: Edmund G. Love (Collier's, September 6, 1952); Director of Photography: Charles G. Clarke A.S.C.; Art Direction: Lyle Wheeler and Lewis Creber; Set Decoration: Al Orenbach; Technicolor Color Consultant: Leonard Doss; Editor: Robert Fritch, A.C.E.; Wardrobe Direction: Charles Le Maire; Music: Sol Kaplan; Orchestration: Edward Powell; Makeup: Ben Nye; Special Photographic Effects: Ray Kellogg; Sound: Arhut L. Kirbach and Harry M. Leonard; Assistant Director: J. Richard Mayberry; Production Managers: R. L. Hough; Technical Advisor: Richard Rudolph, University of California at Los Angeles. Color by Technicolor. 89 minutes.

Cast: Richard Widmark (Sam McHale); Don Taylor (Jenkins); Casey Adams (Walter Landers); Murvyn Vye (Kengtu); Darryl Hickman (Wilbur Cohen); Martin Milner (Elwood Halsey); Ross Bagdasarian (Paul Sabatello); Judy Dann (Nura-Salu); Rodolfo Acosta (Tomec); Russell Collins (Commander Wyatt); Leonard Strong (Wali-Akham); Earl Holliman (Frank Swenson); Anthony Earl Numkena (Son of Kengtu); Edgar Barrier (Yin Tang); Alvy Moore (Aide); Willis Bouchey (Captain Gates); Stuart Randall (Captain Briggs); William Forrest (Skipper); Bert Moorhouse (Naval Captain); Jack Raine (Admiral); Richard Allan (Naval Officer); Frank Iwanaga (Lieutenant); Rollin Moriyama (Cavalry Man); Edo Mita (Lieutenant Colonel); Frank Kumagi (Jap); Harris Matsushige (Jap Officer); Beal Wong (Jap Naval Officer); William Self (Lieutenant); Russ Conway (Operations); Ray Montgomery, John Hedloe, Leo Needham (Pilots); James Conaty (Admiral); Franklyn Farnum (General); Richard Loo (Jap Major); Rush Williams (M.P.); Robert Kino (Jap Officer).

Reviews: "A gripping tale of hard adventure...an absorbing, finely acted and skillfully directed melodrama of World War II, rich in stirring action and rugged humor." (Hollywood Reporter, February 19, 1953).

Notes: Working title: Sixty Saddles For Gobi. 20th Century-Fox press material called the film "10 per cent factual, 90 per cent fictional and 100 per cent dynamic." Edmund Love's original Collier's story was about the teams of Armed Forces weather observers stationed in the Gobi during World War II. Local Mongol tribes offered important assistance and friendship and, in gratitude, 90 saddles were flown in from the United States for presentation to the Mongols. For unknown reasons, the 90 saddles became 60 saddles in the film.

The Gobi desert scenes were filmed at Nixon, Nevada, on the shores of Pyramid Lake. Technical Advisor Richard Rudolph claimed that not only did the Nevada wastelands resemble the Gobi but that the local Piute Indians bore "an extraordinary resemblance" to Mongol tribesman. The cast and crew were headquartered about fifty miles away in Reno, at the Mapes Hotel and River House. A few exteriors were also filmed in Fallon, Nevada. Interiors and the scenes in the Chinese walled town were shot on the 20th Century-Fox back lot in Century City.

F38   THE DESERT RATS (1953).

    20th Century-Fox

    Produced by Robert L. Jacks. DIRECTED BY ROBERT WISE. Screenplay: Richard Murphy; Director of Photography: Lucien Ballard, A.S.C.; Art Direction: Lyle Wheeler and Addison Hehr; Set Decoration: Fred J. Rodo; Editor: Barbara McLean, A.C.E.; Music: Leigh Harline; Wardrobe Direction: Charles Le Maire; Musical Director: Alfred Newman; Orchestration: Edward Powell; Makeup Artist: Ben Nye; Sound: Alfred Bruzlin and Roger Heman; Assistant Director: J. Richard Mayberry. 88 minutes.

    Cast: Michael Rennie (Narrator); Richard Burton (Captain MacRoberts); James Mason (Rommel); Robert Newton (Bartlett): Robert Douglas (General); Torin Thatcher (Barney); Chips Rafferty (Sgt. Smith); Charles Tingwell (Lt. Carstairs); Charles Davis (Pete); Ben Wright (Mick); James Lilburn (Communications Man); John O'Malley (Riley); Ray Harden (Hugh); John Alderson (Corporal); Richard Peel (Rusty); 1 Michael Pate (Captain Currie); Frank Pulaski (Major O'Rourke); Charles Keane (Sgt. Donaldson); Pat O'Moore (Jim); Trevor Constable (Ginger); Albert Taylor (Jensen); John Wengraf (German Doctor); Arno Frey (Kramm); Alfred Zeisler (Von Helmholtz); Charles Fitzsimons (Fire Officer); Noel Drayton (Captain); Gene Darrell (First Aussie); Art Gilmour (Second Aussie); Nick Coster (Medic); Frederick Stevens (German Major); Otto Reichow (Gunner); Jerry Riggio (Commando); Frederick Brune (German Gunner); Frank Chase (Commando); John Blackburn (Sergeant); John Fraser (Artillery Man); Tony Christian (German Sentry); Robert Boon (German Lieutenant); Per Skavlan (German Guard); Paul V. Busch (German Orderly); Harold Dyrenforth (Observer); Lester Matthews (Foreign Secretary); Jack Raine (C.I.C.); Clyde Morris (British Communications Man); Arthur Brunner (German Radio Man); Ashley Cowan (Corporal); Pat Aherne (English Officer); Gilchrist Stuart (Captain); Peter Ortiz (Wireman); Gavin Muir (Captain); Paul Cavanaugh (Colonel);

Awards: Academy Award nomination for Richard Murphy's story and screenplay.

Reviews: "Director Robert Wise has gotten an almost documentary quality into his action sequences. It's combat history brought alive with spine-tingling realism." (Arthur Knight, Saturday Review, May 16, 1953).

"...first-rate production values, and director Robert Wise's direction is sufficiently spirited, but there are times when the picture lacks a certain continuity, appearing almost episodic." (Howard McCaly, Los Angeles Daily News, May 7, 1953).

Notes: Filmed in November and December, 1952 near Borrego Springs, California. James Mason had already played Rommel in Henry Hathaway's The Desert Fox (1951).

Video Availability: Fox Video, Facets Multimedia.

F39   SO BIG (1953).

Warner Bros.

Produced by Henry Blanke. DIRECTED BY ROBERT WISE. Screenplay: John Twist. From the novel by Edna Ferber. Director of Photography: Ellsworth Fredricks; Dialogue Director: Tony Jowitt; Assistant Director: Russ Saunders; 2nd Assistant Director: Fred Sheld; Camera Operator: Harry Davis; Assistant Cameraman: Stewart Higgs; Script Supervisor: Irva Mae Ross; Art Director: John Beckman; Set Decorator: George Hopkins; Editor: Thomas Reilly; Sound: Oliver Garrettson; Propman: Bud Friend; Assistant Propman: George Sweeney; Gaffer: Paul Burnett; Best Boy: Ed Rike; Grip: Hershal Brown; Makeup: Edward Allane; Hair Dresser: Betty Lou Delmont; Wardrobe Woman: Rudy Harrington; Wardrobe Man: Jack Delaney; Music: Max Steiner. 101 minutes.

Cast: Jane Wyman (Selina DeJong); Sterling Hayden (Pervus DeJong); Nancy Olson (Dallas O'Mara); Steve Forrest (Dirk DeJong); Elisabeth Fraser (Julie Hempel); Martha Hyer (Paula Hempel); Walter Coy (Roelf Pool); Richard Beymer (Roelf, aged 12); Tommy Rettig (Dirk, aged 8); Roland Winters (Klaas Pool); Jacques Aubuchon (August Hempel); Ruth Swanson (Maartje Pool); Dorothy Christy (Widow

Paarlenberg); Noralee Norman (Geertje Pool); Jill Janssen (Jozina Pool); Kerry Donnelly (Paula, aged 8); Kenneth Osmond (Eugene, aged 9); Lotte Stein (Meana); Arthur Fox (Dirk, aged 3); Vera Miles, Evan Loew, Frances Osborne, Jean Garvin, Carol Grei (Girls); Lily Kemble Cooper (Miss Fister); Grandon Rhodes (Bainbridge); Anthony Jochim (Accountant); Herb Vigran (Boss); Joe Du Val (Jakob);Oliver Blake (Adam Coms); Frank Kreig, Bob Stephenson, Paul Brinegar, Billy Vincent (Bidders); George Selk (Johnnes Ambuul); Spec O'Donnell (Man in Chair); John Maxwell (Rev. Dekker); Sara Taft (Woman); Bud Osborne (Wagon Driver); Ray Bennett (Al); Dorothy Granger (1st Lady); Elizabeth Russell (2nd Lady); Jennings Miles (Seller); Frank Chase, Phil Tead, John Logan, James Stone (Buyers); Marjorie Bennett (Woman Servant); Bill O'Brien (Man Servant); David McMahon (Policeman); Charlicie Garrett (Cook); Joy Hallward (Maid); Bill Grimes, Thor Holmes, Michael Pierce, Clay Bennett (Bits); Cathy Creighton, Sue George, Gloria Moore, Jeanetta Lewis (Bits); Frank Ferguson (Assistant); Tom Royal (Eugene); Lillian Culver (Mrs. Robinson); Douglas Evans (Richard Hollis); Mary Alan Hokanson (Secretary); Joe Brooks, Mike Lally, Jack Henderson, Ralph Volkie, Steve Stephan, Al Loyd, John Konorez, Dan Dowling, Dick Alexander, James Dime (Bidders); Chalky Williams (Policeman); Abdullah Abbas (Hawker); Jon Provost (Dirk, aged 2); Kenner G. Kemp (Hempel's Chauffeur).

Reviews: "Robert Wise couldn't overcome a rambling, unexciting script, a factor that is certainly not to the discredit of this promising young director." (Nat Kahn, Hollywood Reporter, September 30, 1953).

Notes: Filmed previously in 1924 by Charles Brabin and 1932 by William A. Wellman. While strictly a coincidence, it is interesting to note that Dirk at different stages of childhood is played by the two young actors who co-starred, at different times, with Lassie on television in the 1950s: Tommy Rettig and Jon Provost.

F40 EXECUTIVE SUITE (1954).

M-G-M.

Produced by John Houseman. DIRECTED BY ROBERT WISE. Associate Producer: Jud Kinberg; Screenplay: Ernest Lehman. From the novel by Cameron Hawley. Director of Photography: George Folsey, A.S.C.; Art Direction: Cedric Gibbons and Edward Carfagno; Editor:

Ralph E. Winters, A.C.E.; Assistant Director: George Rhein; Recording Supervisor: Douglas Shearer; Set Decoration: Edwin B. Willis and Emile Kuri; Special Effects: A. Arnold Gillespie and Warren Newcombe; Women's Costumes Designed by: Helen Rose; Hair Styles: Sydney Guillaroff; Makeup: William Tuttle. 106 minutes.

Cast: William Holden (McDonald Walling); June Allyson (Mary Blemond Walling); Barbara Stanwyck (Julia O. Treadway); Fredric March (Loren Phineas Shaw); Walter Pidgeon (Frederick Y. Alderson); Shelley Winters (Eva Bardeman); Paul Douglas (Josiah Walter Dudley); Louis Calhern (George Nyle Caswell); Dean Jagger (Jesse O. Grimm); Nina Foch (Erica Martin); Tim Considine (Mike Walling); Lucille Knoch (Mrs. Caswell); Edgar Stehli (Julius Steigel); William Phipps (Bill Lundeen); Mary Adams (Sara Asenath Grimm); Virginia Brissac (Edith Alderson); Harry Shannon (Ed Benedeck); Charles Wagenheim (Luigi Cassoni); Virginia Eiler (Western Union Operator); Jonathan Cott (Cop); Robin Camp (Mailroom Boy); Ray Mansfield (Alderson Secretary); A. Cameron Grant (Salesman); Bert Davidson (Salesman); May McAvoy (Grimm Secretary); Willis Bouchey, John Doucette (Morgue Officials); Esther Michelson (News Dealer); Gus Schilling (News Dealer); Abe Dinovitch (Cab Driver); Faith Geer (Hat Check Girl); Mimi Doyle (Telephone Operator); Mary Alan Hokanson (Nurse); Paul Bryar (Waiter); John Banner (Enrique); Roy Engel (Jimmy Farrell); Madie Norman (Wailing Housekeeper); Dan Riss (City Editor); David McMahon (First Reporter); Ralph Montgomery (Second Reporter); Bernice Simmons, Helen Dickson, Nesdon Booth, Hugh Boswell (Guests); Lucile Curtis (Maid); Raoul Freeman (Avery Bullard); Bob Carson (Lee Ormond); John Hedloe (Reporter); Ann Tyrell (Shaw Secretary); Carl Saxe, Dick Landry, Tom McDonough (Workers); Kazia Orzazewski (Old Woman "Liz"); Burt Mustin (Sam Teal); Helen Brown (Miss Clark); John McKee (Umpire); Jack Gargan, George Sherwood, Jerry Sheldon, Gene Coogan, Darren Dublin (Ad Libs); Wilson Wood (Airport Clerk); Phil Chambers (Toll Station Attendant); Matt Moore (Servant); Mike Lally (Spectator at Ball Game).

Awards and Nominations: Executive Suite received Academy Award nominations for Supporting Actress (Nina Foch); Black-and-White Cinematography; Black-and-White Art Direction-Set Decoration; Black-and-White Costume Design.

National Board of Review Awards: Supporting Actress (Nina Foch); The Board named Executive Suite one of the Ten Best American Films of 1954. Venice Film Festival Prize: Special Jury Prize for Ensemble

Acting.

Reviews: "Here is a magnificent motion picture that meets the standard of greatness on almost every count. Superbly directed by Robert Wise...it is one of the outstanding motion pictures of recent years." (Milton Luban, Hollywood Reporter, February 23, 1954).

Notes: Executive Suite became a television series in 1976, produced by MGM-TV and starring Mitchell Ryan, Stephen Elliott, Sharon Acker and Leigh McCloskey. Stanley Rubin and Norman Felton produced.

Video Availability: MGM/UA Home Video.

F41 HELEN OF TROY (1955).

Warner Bros.

DIRECTED BY ROBERT WISE. Screenplay: John Twist and Hugh Gray; Adaptation: Hugh Gray and N. Richard Nash; Director of Photography: Harry Stradling; Second Unit Director (uncredited): Raoul Walsh; Special Photographic Effects: Louis Lichtenfield; Art Director: Edward Carrere; Production Design and Third Unit Director: Maurice Zuberano; Editor: Thomas Reilly; Music: Max Steiner; Production Managers: Maurizi Lodi-Fe and Giuseppi de Blasio; Costumes: Roger Furse; Stunt Coordinator: Yakima Canutt; Assistant Director: Gus Agosti; Choreography: Madi Obolensky. WarnerColor. CinemaScope. Stereophonic Sound. 114 minutes.

Cast: Rossana Podesta (Helen); Jack [Jacques] Sernas (Paris); Sir Cedric Hardwicke (Priam); Stanley Baker (Achilles); Niall MacGinnis (Menalaus); Robert Douglas (Agamemnon); Nora Swinburne (Hecuba); Torin Thatcher (Ulysses); Harry Andrews (Hector); Janetto Scott (Cassandra); Ronald Lewis (Aeneas); Brigitte Bardot (Andraste); Guido Notari (Nestor); Eduarde Ciannelli (Andros); Marc Lawrence (Diomedes); Maxwell Reed (Ajax); Robert Brown (Polydorus); Barbara Cavan (Cora); Terence Longden (Patroclus); Patricia Marmont (Andromache); Tonio Stewart (Adelphous); George Zoritch (Dancer); Esmond Knight (High Priest).

Reviews: "Wise handles his crowds and spectacle with a firm hand, drawing the audience always into the very heart of every shot, filling the CinemaScope screen with splendid action and yet unmistakably highlighting each significant detail." (Saturday Review, January 28, 1956).

"Robert Wise, whose direction of Executive Suite was so notable, seems completely out of harmony with his subject matter." (Hollywood Reporter, December 21, 1955).

"Out-sized all the way, Helen makes use of tremendous sets and mob scenes to maintain its hugeness. On this score, it's successful, but it takes more than size alone to hold an audience for 114 minutes. What [Wise] does with his crowd scenes is top flight." (Variety, December 21, 1955).

Notes: Filmed in Italy's Mediterranean area on an unoccupied stretch of land between Rome and the sea at Ostia and at CineCitta Studios in Rome. According to a February, 1956 lawsuit, Helen of Troy was brought to Warner Bros. in 1951 by producer Samuel Bischoff. Bischoff's original script, entitled Atalanta, was written by Hugh Gray, N. Richard Nash and John Twist. Michael Curtiz was signed to direct. When Wise replaced Curtiz and the production moved from Hollywood to Rome, Bischoff was summarily dismissed. He and the writers sued. The writers, at least, were reinstated and given screen credit.

The wooden Trojan Horse was, according to studio publicity, forty feet high and weighed more than eighty tons. Thirty full-grown trees -- fir, beech and poplar -- were used in its construction and it was held together by more than a thousand pounds of nails, plus a "wagon load" of screws, wooden pegs and iron rings. It sat upon a platform sixty feet long and rolled forward on wheels eight feet in diameter and two feet thick. Twenty-five men could fit inside, which was air conditioned.

It was announced in The Hollywood Reporter (August 6, 1953) that Helen of Troy would be filmed in Warner SuperScope, a 70mm process. It was eventually filmed in conventional 35mm CinemaScope.

On August 18, 1954, while two thousand extras broke for lunch, fire swept through a two acre reproduction of Troy, destroying 80% of the sets. The damage was estimate at $160,000. Firemen blamed the blaze on a cigarette.

Helen of Troy was based upon Homer's Iliad. Other film

versions of the story include The Private Life of Helen of Troy (1927); The Queen of Sparta (1931); Loves of Three Queens (a.k.a. The Face That Launched a Thousand Ships, 1953); The Trojan Horse (1962).

F42   TRIBUTE TO A BAD MAN (1956).

    M-G-M.

    Produced by Sam Zimbalist. DIRECTED BY ROBERT WISE. Screenplay: Michael Blankfort. From the short story "Jeremy Rodock" by Jack Schaefer. Director of Photography: Robert Surtees, A.S.C.; Art Direction: Cedric Gibbons and Paul Groesse; Set Decoration: Edwin B. Willis and Fred MacLean; Editor: Ralph E. Winters, A.C.E.; Music: Miklos Rozsa; Recording Supervisor: Dr. Wesley C. Miller; Costumes for Irene Papas by Walter Plunkett; Color Consultant: Charles K. Hagedon; Assistant Director: Arvid Griffin; Hair Styles: Sydney Guilaroff; Makeup: William Tuttle. Eastman Color. CinemaScope. 95 minutes.

    Cast: James Cagney (Jeremy Rodock); Don Dubbins (Steve Miller); Stephen McNally (McNulty); Irene Papas (Jocasta Constantine); Vic Morrow (Lars Peterson); Royal Dano (Abe);James Bell (L.A. Peterson); Jeanette Nolan (Mrs. L.A. Peterson); Lee Van Cleef (Fat Jones); James Griffith (Barjak); Chubby Johnson (Baldy); Onslow Stevens (Hearn); Peter Chong (Cookey); James McCallion (Shorty); Clint Sharp (Red); Carl Pitti (Tom); Tony Hughes (Buyer #1); Roy Engel (Buyer #2); Bud Osborne, John Halloran, Tom London, Dennis Moore, Buddy Roosevelt, Billy Dix (Cowboys).

    Notes: The film was started on location in Colorado with Spencer Tracy in the leading role. After four days of filming, on June 25, 1955, Tracy was fired. The official line was that the filming was too strenuous for Tracy but actually he had forced his own removal due to disagreements over the script and location filming. His removal ended Tracy's twenty-five year residence at M-G-M.

    "James Cagney was one of three or four actors who were discussed as replacements for Spencer," Wise said. [A59]. "[Clark] Gable was definitely approached about it but he didn't want to do it. We finally made a commitment with Cagney but he couldn't do it immediately so we had to shut down and resume again in two months. We made a few adjustments to the script but no major re-writes because [Tracy and Cagney] were not dissimilar physically."

Production was held up again when actor Bob Francis, a student pilot, was killed in a plane crash on July 3, 1955. All scenes featuring Francis were re-shot with Don Dubbins.

"Fat Jones" was the name of a horse wrangler who supplied mounts to the studio. Lee Van Cleef's use of the name in this film may be an in-joke.

F43 SOMEBODY UP THERE LIKES ME (1956).

M-G-M.

Executive Producer: Dore Schary. Produced by Charles Schnee. DIRECTED BY ROBERT WISE. Associate Producer: James E. Newcom; Screenplay: Ernest Lehman. From the autobiography by Rocky Graziano written with Rowland Barber. Director of Photography: Joseph Ruttenberg, A.S.C.; Art Direction: Cedric Gibbons and Malcolm Brown; Set Decoration: Edwin B. Willis and Keogh Gleason; Editor: Albert Akst, A.C.E.; Assistant Director: Robert Saunders; Music: Bronislau Kaper; Title Song, Lyrics by Sammy Cahn, Music by Bronislau Kaper and Sung by Perry Como; Recording Supervisor: Dr. Wesley C. Miller; Makeup: William Tuttle; Technical Advisor: Johnny Indrisano. 110 minutes.

Cast: Paul Newman (Rocky Graziano); Pier Angeli (Norma Levine Graziano); Everett Sloane (Irving Cohen); Eileen Heckart (Ma Barbella); Sal Mineo (Romolo); Harold J. Stone (Nick Barbella); Joseph Buloff (Benny); Sammy White (Whitey Bimstein); Arch Johnson (Heldon); Robert Loggia (Frankie Peppo); Judson Pratt (Johnny Hyland); Matt Crowley (Lou Stillman); Harry Wismer and Sam Taub (Announcers); Donna Jo Gribble (Yolanda Barbella); Robert Easton (Cpl. Eggleston); Ray Stricklyn (Bryson); John Rosser and Frank Campanella (Detectives); Ralph Vitti (Shorty); Robert Lieb (Questioner); Theodore Newton (Commissioner Eddie Eagan); Steve McQueen (Fidel); Willard Sage (Captain); Stanley Adams (Lawyer); James O'Rear (Judge); James Todd (Colonel); Jack Kelk (George); Russ Conway (Captain Grifton); Courtland Shepard (Tony Zale); Terry Rangno (Rocky, aged 8); Pat Lawless (1st Policeman); Joe McGuinn (2nd Policeman); Jan Gillum (Yolande, aged 12); Bern Hoffman (Fat Man); Bill Nelson (Driver); George Cisar (Fence); Walter Cartier (Polack); Sam Gilman (Detective); Jack Kenney, Jack Lomas (Guards); John Eldredge (Warden Niles); Dick Rich (Guard); Eddie Ryder (Prisoner); Clancy Cooper (Captain Lancheck); Gregg Martell (Guard); John Rosser (1st Detective); Frank

Campanella (2nd Detective); Dean Jones (Private); Ray Stricklyn (Bryson); Ralph Reed (Soldier); Wayne Taylor (Prisoner); Caswell Adams (Sam); Andy Savilia, Philip Morini, Bob Gardette (Reporters); Benny Rubin (Man); Jimmy Murphy (Fighter); Ben Cameron (Man); William Boyett (M.P.); Tony Michaels (Assistant Commissioner); Vincent Correccio (Tough Kid); Charles Green (Curtis Hightower); Don Shelton (Captain); Don Haggerty, Walter Johnson, Jack Shea (Guards); Tyler McVey, Len Lesser (Reporters); Jack Orrison (Detective); Robin Morse (Man); Byron Kane, Jesse Kirkpatric, Paul Weber (Reporters); Sid Raymond (Subway Guard); Tommy White (Boy); Al Silvani (Rocky's Second); Angela Cartwright (Audrey, aged 5); David Leonard (Mr. Mueller); Bart Bradley (Boy); Michael Ross (Policeman); Russ Clark (Zale Fight Referee); Joe Costa (Racketeer); Renata Vanni (Woman); Joe Marr (Customer); Michael Bookasta (Boy at Parade); Walter Beaver, Brad Slaven (Sidekicks); Ben Moselle (Referee at Army Arena); Joe LaBarba (Brooklyn Referee; Billy Nelson (Commissioner); Rodney Jones, Pete Gonzales (Fighters); Frank Neckero, Ralph Neff, Sam Scar, Harry Arnie (Spectators); Cy Malis, Dynamite Jackson, Tom Garland (Referees); Ray Walker (Ring Announcer).

Awards: Academy Awards for Cinematography (Black-and-White) and Art Direction and Set Decoration (Black-and-White).

For once the Harvard Lampoon's "Movie Worsts" Awards had something good to say about a Wise film, naming Somebody Up There Likes Me as one of "The Best Alternative[s] to The Ten Commandments."

Golden Globes: Paul Newman, Tony Perkins and John Kerr were named Most Promising Newcomers -- Male.

The National Board of Review named Somebody Up There Likes Me as one of the year's Ten Best films.

Reviews: "...a genuinely artistic film that also has all the ingredients of popular acclaim and acceptance...one of the most jolting, absorbing and moving pictures ever made." (Hollywood Reporter, July 5, 1956).

"Direction by Robert Wise is strong, standard and very effective. You can say of it that it escapes notice, permitting you to pay attention to the story being told. And that's enough. It's a story that shakes you." (Archer Winsten, The New York Post, July 6, 1956).

Notes: James Dean was originally cast in the role of Rocky Graziano. According to Dore Schary's autobiography Heyday, when Metro-Goldwyn-Mayer loaned Elizabeth Taylor to Warner Bros. for Giant (1956), the studio obtained Dean's services from Warners for one picture in return. On the day after Dean's first meeting with Schary about the film, he was killed in an automobile accident. Wise said that he never met Dean but always preferred Paul Newman in the role. "I always had in my mind that maybe Dean was not physically a middleweight, somehow. And Paul did one of his best characterizations in it; he really caught that man." [A132]

Video Availability: MGM/UA Home Video.

F44   THIS COULD BE THE NIGHT (1957).

M-G-M.

Produced by Joe Pasternak. DIRECTED BY ROBERT WISE. Screenplay: Isobel Lennart; From the stories "Protection for a Tough Racket" and "It's Hard to Find Mecca" by Cordelia Baird Gross; Director of Photography: Russell Harlan; Art Direction: William A. Horning and Paul Groesse; Set Decoration: Edwin B. Willis and Robert R. Benton; Editor: George Boemler; Music Director: George Stoll; Musical Numbers Staged by: Jack Baker; Sound: Dr. Wesley C. Miller. CinemaScope. 104 minutes.

Songs: "This Could Be The Night," "Hustlin' News Gal," and "I Got It Bad" by Duke Ellington and Paul Francis Webster; "I'm Gonna Live Till I Die" by Al Hoffman, Walter Kent, and Mann Curtis; "Taking a Chance on Love" by John Latouche, Ted Fetter and Vernon Duke; "Blue Moon" by Richard Rodgers and Lorenz Hart; "Dream Dancing" by Cole Porter; "The Tender Trap" by Sammy Cahn and Jimmy Van Heusen; "Trumpet Boogie" and "Mamba Combo" (anon).

Cast: Jean Simmons (Anne Leeds); Paul Douglas (Rocco); Anthony Franciosa (Tony Armotti); Julie Wilson (Ivy Corlane); Joan Blondell (Crystal); Neile Adams (Patsy St. Clair); J. Carroll Naish (Leon); Rafael Campos (Hussein Mohammed); ZaSu Pitts (Mrs. Shea); Tom Helmore (Stowe Devlin); Murvyn Vye (Waxie London); Vaughn Taylor (Ziggy Dawlt); Frank Ferguson (Mr. Shea); William Ogden Joyce (Bruce Cameron); James Todd (Mr. Hallerby); Ray Anthony and his Orchestra; John Harding (Eduardo); Percy Helton (Charlie); Richard Collier (Homer);

Edna Holland (Teacher); Betty Uitti (Sexy Girl); Lew Smith (Waiter); June Blair (Chorus Girl); Charles Wagenheim (Mike, Bartender); Sid Kane, E. Molinari, Bruno Della Santina (Waiters); Francesca Bellini (Flashy Woman); Paul Peterson (Joey); Gloria Pall (New Girl); Harry Hines, Gregg Martell, Matty Fain (Mug Guests); Carol LeVegue (Girl); Ray Walker (M.C.); Nora Marlowe (Mrs. Gretcham); Billy McLean (Man Contestant); Tim Graham (Official); Leonard Strong (Mr. Bernbaum); Mel Dowd (Girl's Voice); Len Lesser (Piano Tuner); Bobby Kanner, Bobby Diamond, Bart Bradley, Billy Stoll, Jeff Jarvis, Jon Jarvis (Boys in Class); Robin Morse (Man); Lennie Bremen (Dealer); Frank Kreig (1st Drunk); Billy Nelson (2nd Drunk); Sid Melton (Taxi Driver); Don Anderson (Waiter Captain); Boy Foy, Lilly Steels ("The Boys" Act); Archie Savage, Andrew Robinson, Walter Davis (Archie Savage Trio).

Reviews: "The charming and witty screenplay...is a Runyonesque fable of guys and dolls along the Broadway beat...Wise has expertly guided this rather delicate form with sense and sensitivity." (James Powers, Hollywood Reporter, April 9, 1957)

Notes: Working title: Protection for a Tough Racket.

Video Availability: MGM/UA Home Video.

F45 UNTIL THEY SAIL (1957).

M-G-M.

Produced by Charles Schnee. DIRECTED BY ROBERT WISE. Associate Producer: James E. Newcom; Screenplay: Robert Anderson; from the story in the collection "Return to Paradise" by James A. Michener; Director of Photography: Joseph Ruttenberg, A.S.C.; Art Direction: William A. Hornung and Paul Groesse; Set Decoration: Edwin B. Willis, Henry Grace; Special Effects: A. Arnold Gillespie and Lee LeBlanc; Recording Supervisor: Dr. Wesley C. Miller; Assistant Director: Ridgeway Callow; Hairstyles: Sydney Guillaroff; Makeup: William Tuttle; Editor: Harold F. Kress; Music: David Raksin; Song "Until They Sail," Lyrics by Sammy Cahn, Sung by Eydie Gorme. CinemaScope. Perspecta Sound. Westrex Recording System. 95 minutes.

Cast: Jean Simmons (Barbara Leslie Forbes); Joan Fontaine (Anne Leslie); Paul Newman (Capt. Jack Harding); Piper Laurie (Delia Leslie); Charles Drake (Capt. Richard G. Bates); Sandra Dee (Evelyn

Leslie); Wally Cassell ("Shiner" Phil Friskett); Alan Napier (Prosecution); Ralph Votrian (Max Murphy); John Wilder (Tommy); Tige Andrews (Marine); Adam Kennedy (Lt. Andy); Mickey Shaughnessy (Marine); Patrick Macnee (Private Duff); Ben Wright (Defense); Kendrick Huxham (Justice); James Todd (Consul); David Thursby (Trainman); Hilda Plowright (Woman); Nicky Blair (1st Marine); Morgan Jones (2nd Marine); Jack Mann (Sergeant); Molly Glessing (Hotel Clerk); Pat Waltz, William Boyett, Jimmy Hayes (Marines); Alex Frazer (Mr. Hall); John Dennis (Sergeant); George Pelling (Steward); Owen McGiveney (Bank Official); Dean Jones (Marine Lieutenant); Robert Keys (Major Campbell); Ann Wakefield (Mrs. Campbell); Rush Williams, Lee Rhodes, James Douglas (Marine Officers); Alma Lauton (1st New Zealand Girl); Dee Humphrey (2nd New Zealand Girl); Jay Douglas, Pat Colby, Dan Eitner (Bit Marines); Jacqueline Terry, June Mitchell (New Zealand Girls); Tom Mayton, Roger McGee, John Rosser, Jim Cox (Marines); Dorris Riter, Pamela Light, Phyllis Douglas, Jennifer Raine (Girls); Vesey O'Davoren (Bit Minister); Pat O'Hara (Police Inspector); Stanley Fraser (Court Crier).

Video Availability: MGM/UA Home Video.

F46   RUN SILENT, RUN DEEP (1958).

United Artists. A Hecht-Hill Lancaster Production/ Jeffrey Production.

Produced by Harold Hecht. DIRECTED BY ROBERT WISE. Associate Producer: William Schorr; Screenplay: John Gay; From the novel by Commander Edward L. Beach; Director of Photography: Russell Harlan; Art Director: Edward Carrere; Editor: George Boemler; Music: Franz Waxman. 93 minutes.

Cast: Clark Gable (Commander "Rich" Richardson); Burt Lancaster (Lt. Jim Bledsoe); Jack Warden (Mueller); Brad Dexter (Cartwright); Don Rickles (Ruby); Nick Cravat (Russo);Joe Maross (Kohler); Mary La Roche (Laura Richardson); Eddie Foy III (Larto); Rudy Bond (Cullen); H.M. Wynant (Hendrix); John Bryant (Beckman); Joel Fluellen (Bragg); Jimmie Bates (Jessie); Ken Lynch (Frank); John Gibson (Captain Blunt); Tom Riley (Carver); John Close (Lieutenant).

Notes: The U.S.S. Redfish of Submarine Division 32 plays the Nerke.

Reviews: The Hollywood Reporter called Run Silent, Run Deep, "An adult and intelligent adventure drama." (March 24, 1958).

"Director Robert Wise has maintained a top degree of suspense." (Dick Williams, The Los Angeles Mirror-News, April 3, 1958).

Video Availability: CBS/Fox Video, Facets Multimedia.

F47   I WANT TO LIVE! (1958).

United Artists. A Figaro Production.

Produced by Walter Wanger. DIRECTED BY ROBERT WISE. Screenplay: Nelson Gidding and Don Mankiewicz; From articles by Ed Montgomery and Letters of Barbara Graham; Director of Photography: Lionel Lindon, A.S.C.; Art Director: Ted Haworth; Editor: William Hornbeck, A.C.E.; Assistant Director: George Vieira; Music: John Mandel; Jazz performed by Gerry Mulligan, Shelly Manne, Art Farmer, Bud Shank, Red Mitchell, Frank Rosolino, Pete Jolly; Set Decoration: Victor Gangelin; Costumes: Wes Jeffries and Angela Alexander; Makeup: Tom Tuttle and Jack Stone; Hair Stylists: Emmy Eckhardt and Lilliam Hokom Ugrin; Script Supervisor: Stanley Scheuer. 120 minutes.

Cast: Susan Hayward (Barbara Graham); Simon Oakland (Ed Montgomery); Virginia Vincent (Peg); Theodore Bikel (Carl Palmberg); Wesley Lau (Henry Graham); Philip Coolidge (Emmett Perkins); Lou Krugman (Jack Santo); James Philbrook (Bruce King); Bartlett Robinson (D.A.); Gage Clark (Richard G. Tibrow); Joe De Santis (Al Matthews); John Marley (Father Devers); Raymond Bailey (San Quentin Warden); Alice Backes (San Quentin Nurse); Gertrude Flynn (San Quentin Matron); Russell Thorson (San Quentin Sergeant); Dabbs Greer (San Quentin Captain); Stafford Repp (Sergeant); Gavin MacLeod (Lieutenant); Peter Breck (Ben Miranda); Marion Marshall (Rita); Olive Blakeney (Corona Warden); Lorna Thayer (Corona Guard); Evelyn Scott (Personal Effects Clerk); Jack Weston (NCO); Leonard Bell (San Francisco Hood); George Putnam (Himself); Bill Stout (Newsman); Jason Johnson (Bixel); Rusty Lane (Judge); S. John Launer (San Quentin Officer); Dan Sheridan (Police Broadcaster); Wendell Holmes (Detective).

Reviews: "...Robert Wise's direction has extraordinary pace and style, from the staccato movement of the first part to the cold, precision tempo toward the end. He keeps it hard, with an almost documentary sharpness..." (Bosley Crowther, The New York Times, November 23, 1958).

"To judge from the far-out photography, real desperate sound track, and dragsville dialogue...Producer Walter Wanger seems less concerned to assist the triumph of justice than to provide the morbid market with a sure-enough gasser." (Time, November 24, 1958).

Awards: Academy Award: Best Actress (Susan Hayward). Academy Award Nominations: BEST DIRECTOR (Robert Wise); Best Screenplay (Based on Material From Another Medium); Black-and-White Cinematography; Sound; Film Editing.

New York Film Critics Award: Best Actress (Susan Hayward).

Golden Globe Award: Best Actress--Drama (Susan Hayward).

Harvard Lampoon's "Movie Worsts" Award: "Most Unreasonable Request": Susan Hayward in I Wanna Live [sic]."

I Want To Live! was named as one of the The New York Times' Ten Best Films of 1958.

Notes: I Want To Live! was originally banned in Great Britain and only released when some five minutes of the execution sequence were excised. John Trevelyan, secretary of the British Film Board, explained their objections: "We have always felt that taking life by execution is not a fit subject for entertainment."

Barbara Graham was convicted and executed (along with accomplices Jack Santo and Emmett Perkins) for her alleged participation in the 1953 murder of Mabel Monahan, an elderly Burbank woman. Graham died on June 3, 1955. To drive home the brutality -- and, he believed, uselessness -- of the death penalty, Wise was determined to present her execution in grim, minute detail. He and his staff visited San Quentin prison where officials showed them the step-by-step procedure of gassing someone to death. Wise took photographs of the death cell and gas chamber so that they could be reproduced perfectly in the studio.

Feeling that even this attention to detail wasn't enough, Wise finally requested that he be allowed to witness an execution. With the warden, a doctor and two witnesses, Wise watched a young man, convicted of two murders, die in the gas chamber. "That boy wasn't emotional about dying," Wise said. "He was stunned, rather knocked out." The doctor explained to the director that this was often the case, that people have a safety valve that takes over at moments of unbearable stress, serving to numb the emotions. "So I decided I'd direct Barbara Graham's death without emotion, without hysterics." The execution scene alone took two and a half weeks to shoot. The experience was emotionally exhausting for both Wise and Susan Hayward.

The first draft of the script was written by Don Mankiewicz, nephew of famed screenwriter-director-producer Joseph Mankiewicz. Wise felt that Mankiewicz's effort was unsuccessful and writer Nelson Gidding was brought in to rewrite the script. A Writers' Guild arbitration determined that Mankiewicz should receive a co-writing credit with Gidding but, Wise said, "I don't think he really deserved it. Don's draft was done before I was on the picture and I didn't like it at all. I only took the project on the condition that we get another writer and get a new script." [A59] I Want To Live! marked the first of several collaborations between Wise and Gidding, including Odds Against Tomorrow, The Haunting and The Andromeda Strain and The Hindenburg.

Although Wise and Gidding were careful not to take a position in the film regarding Graham's guilt or innocence, police and prosecutors who worked on the Graham case were appalled by what they considered the film's stance: that Graham was unjustly convicted of murder. Dan Lundberg, a Los Angeles newsman and television announcer, and writer Hugh Lacy announced that they were planning another film about the case to be called Weep No More For Barbara. Lundberg and Lacy signed a contract with Deputy District Attorney H. Miller Leavy, who prosecuted Graham, in order to gain access to his files, diary and other documents. Lundberg told Variety (March 4, 1959), "We have documentary proof never before made known of Mrs. Graham's guilt. I Want To Live! is a farce...their effort to show Mrs. Graham was executed although innocent is a monstrous miscarriage. There is overwhelming evidence of her guilt." The team said that Weep No More For Barbara would be told either from the viewpoint of Mabel Monahan or that of the District Attorney.

A year later, Associate Warden Louis Nelson claimed that

Barbara Graham confessed her guilt the night before she was executed to Warden Harley O. Teets. Nelson said (Hollywood Citizen-News, March 11, 1960), "I had...been called to Death Row by a prisoner who wanted to spill his story. He told me a gruesome tale of how he knifed his victim. I couldn't sleep afterwards. It made me ill. The next morning I told Warden Teets about it. I said I didn't think I should have to listen to such things as part of my job. Teets said, 'I know how you feel about it. I had to listen to Barbara Graham tell how she pistol-whipped Mrs. Monahan.'"

Wise, however, objects to the idea that I Want To Live! presents Barbara Graham as innocent. "I myself don't know whether she was innocent or guilty. I can talk to one person who knew her who will say, 'There's no way in the world that she could do such a thing.' Then I'll meet someone else who'll say, 'Oh, if she was high enough or something like that, she might have been capable of murder.' So I don't know. We tried to make it very balanced in the film. The one statement about capital punishment that is in that film is that, no matter what a person has done, no one deserves to be tortured the way Barbara Graham was on the last night of her life. There were quite a few editorials that appeared after her execution that said the same thing." [Interview with Frank Thompson, March 9, 1994].

Video Availability: MGM/UA Home Video (cassette and laser disc; the laser disc contains the original theatrical trailer).

F48   ODDS AGAINST TOMORROW (1959).

United Artists. A Harbel (Harry Belafonte) Production.

PRODUCED AND DIRECTED BY ROBERT WISE. Associate Producer: Phil Stein; Screenplay: Nelson Gidding and John O. Killens (and, uncredited, Abraham Polonsky); From the novel by William P. McGivern; Director of Photography: Joseph Brun; Art Director: Leo Kerz; Editor: Dede Allen; Assistant Director: Charles Maguire; Costumes: Anna Hill Johnstone; Makeup: Robert Jiras; Production Manager: Forrest E. Johnston; Sound: Edward Johnstone and Richard Voriseck; Set Decorator: Fred Ballmeyer; Script Supervisor: Marguerite James; Camera Operator: Sol Midwall; Music: John Lewis. 95 minutes.

Cast: Harry Belafonte (Johnny Ingram); Robert Ryan (Earle Slater); Shelley Winters (Lorry); Ed Begley (Dave Burke); Gloria

Grahame (Helen); Will Kuluva (Bacco); Richard Bright (Coco); Kim Hamilton (Ruth Ingram); Mae Barnes (Annie); Carmen DeLavallade (Kitty); Lou Gallo (Moriarity); Fred J. Scollay (Cannoy); Lois Thorne (Eadie); Wayne Rogers (Soldier); Zohra Lampert (Girl in Bar); William Zuckert (Bartender); Burtt Harris (George); Ed Preble (Hotel Clerk); Mil Stewart (Elevator Operator); Marc May (Ambulance Attendant); Paul Hoffman (Garry); Cicely Tyson (Fra); Robert Jones (Guard at Door--Cannoy's Club); William Adams (Bank Guard); John Garden (Clerk in Bus Station); Allen Nourse (Police Chief of Melton).

Reviews: "...considerable of the credit for its dramatic forcefulness belongs to Robert Wise who [directed] with style. Mood, atmosphere and characterization {make the film] superior to its category as a holdup melodrama." (The Film Daily, October 5, 1959).

"On one level, Odds Against Tomorrow is a taut crime melodrama. On another, it is an allegory about racism, greed and man's propensity for self-destruction. Not altogether successful in the second category, it still succeeds in the first. Produced and directed by Robert Wise with an alert eye and ear to sooty realism the [film] is absorbing [and] disquieting." (Variety, October 2, 1959).

Notes: Odds Against Tomorrow was produced by Harry Belafonte's production company for $1,250,000. It was filmed on location in Hudson, New York and in the Gold Medal Studios in the Bronx.

F49   WEST SIDE STORY (1961).

The Mirisch Company/Seven Arts Productions, Inc./ Beta Productions.

DIRECTED BY ROBERT WISE and Jerome Robbins. PRODUCED BY ROBERT WISE. Screenplay: Ernest Lehman; Based on the play with book by Arthur Laurents; Lyrics: Stephen Sondheim; Music: Leonard Bernstein; As Conceived for the stage, Directed and Choreographed by Jerome Robbins and Produced by Robert E. Griffith and Harold Prince; from the play "Romeo and Juliet" by William Shakespeare; Music Conductor: Johnny Green; Associate producer and music supervisor: Saul Chaplin; Choreography: Jerome Robbins; Director of Photography: Daniel L. Fapp; Assistant Director: Robert E. Relyea; Costume Designer: Irene Sharaff; Assistant Choreographers: Howard Jeffrey, Margaret

Banks, Tommy Abbott, Tony Mordente; Special Photographic Effects and Title Photography: Linwood G. Dunn, Film Effects of Hollywood, Cecil Love, Don Weed; Titles and Visual Consultant: Saul Bass; Production Designer: Boris Leven; Set Decorator: Victor A. Gangelin; Script Supervisor: Stanley Scheuer; Makeup: Emile La Vigne; Hair Stylist: Alice Monte; Film Editor: Thomas Stanford; Assistant Editor: Marshall M. Borden; Production Executives: Marvin Mirisch, Harold Mirisch, Eliot Hyman, Ray Stark; Production Manager: Allen K. Wood; Second Assistant Director: Jerome M. Siegel; Music Assistant: Betty Walberg; Orchestrations: Sid Ramin, Irwin Kostal; Vocal Coach: Robert Tucker; Solo Musicians: Al Viola, Red Mitchell, Jack Dumont, Shelly Manne, Pete Candoli; Music Editor: Richard Carruth; Sound Editor: Gilbert D. Marchant; Sound Supervisors: Gordon E. Sawyer, Fred Hynes; Sound: Murray Spivack, Fred Lau, Vinton Vernon; Re-recording: Samuel Goldwyn Studios and Todd-AO; Wardrobe: Bert Henrikson; Property Master: Sam Gordon; Construction Supervisor: William Maldonado; Casting: Stalmaster-Lister Co.; Title Sequence Camera Operator: John Finger; Title Sequence Dolly Grip: Louis Kulsey; Production Illustrators: Maurice Zuberano, Leon Harris; Negative: Eastman Color. A Mirisch Pictures Inc. presentation in association with Seven Arts Productions Inc. A Beta Production. A BandP Enterprises Picture. A Robert Wise Film. Filmed in Super Panavision 70. Technicolor. Westrex six-track magnetic stereophonic sound. 155 minutes.

Songs and Musical Numbers: "Prologue" (instrumental); "Jet Song" (Tamblyn, Jets); "Something's Coming" (Beymer); "Dance At The Gym" (instrumental); "Tonight" (Beymer, Wood); "Maria" (Beymer); "America" (Chakiris, Moreno, chorus); "One Hand, One Heart" (Beymer, Wood); "Gee, Officer Krupke" (Jets); "The Rumble" (instrumental); "Cool" (Jets); "I Feel Pretty" (Wood, chorus); "Somewhere" (Beymer, Wood); "A Boy Like That/I Have a Love" (Wood, Moreno); "Roof Dance" (Wood).

Cast: Natalie Wood (Maria); Richard Beymer (Tony); Russ Tamblyn (Riff); Rita Moreno (Anita); George Chakiris (Bernardo); Tucker Smith (Ice); Tony Mordente (Action); Eliot Feld (Baby John); David Winters (A-Rab); Bert Michaels (Snowboy); Robert Banas (Joyboy); Anthony "Scooter" Teague (Big Deal); Tommy Abbott (Gee-Tar); Harvey Hohnecker (Mouthpiece); David Bean (Tiger); Sue Oakes (Anybody's); Gina Trikonis (Graziella); Carole D'Andrea (Velma); Jose De Vega (Chino); Jay Norman (Pepe); Gus Trikonis (Indio); Robert Thompson (Luis); Larry Roquemore (Rocco); Jaime Rogers (Loco); Eddie

Verso (Juano); Andre Tayir (Chile); Nick Covvacevich (Toro); Rudy Del Campo (Del Campo); Suzie Kaye (Rosalia); Yvonee Othon (Consuelo); Jo Anne Miya (Francisca); Simon Oakland (Lt. Schrank); Bill Bramley (Officer Krupke); Ned Glass (Doc); John Astin (Glad Hand); Penny Santon (Mme. Lucia); Natalie Wood's Vocals: Marni Nixon; Richard Beymer's Vocals: Jimmy Bryant; Rita Moreno's Vocals: Betty Wand.

Notes: Filmed at Samuel Goldwyn Studios and on location in Los Angeles and New York City. The original stage production of West Side Story opened on Broadway on September 26, 1957 at the Winter Garden. Robert E. Griffith and Harold S. Prince produced and the production was directed and choreographed by Jerome Robbins.

The film was released on October 18, 1961 in roadshow engagements. While most movies at this length contain intermissions, Wise resisted interrupting West Side Story. "It didn't divide," he told Charles Champlin. "I felt that all the tension had to build up consecutively. You can't let the audience up for air for a minute." Many theater owners found a perfect moment for an intermission at the film's mid-point, just before the "I Feel Pretty" number. A long, wordless scene, ending in a musical swell, then a fade-out seems tailor-made for a break. "Some theaters put in an intermission against our instructions," Wise said, "but whenever the studio found out about it, they put a stop to it right away. I put intermissions in The Sound of Music, The Sand Pebbles and Star! because it was appropriate; they were different kinds of movies. But I was adamant about playing West Side Story without a break." [Interview with Frank Thompson, March 9, 1994].

While the film followed the basic structure of the stage show, two numbers were transposed. "Cool" originally took place in the first act and "Officer Krupke" in the second. Wise told John Gallagher, "We always felt that the 'Krupke' number, the funny number the kids do in front of the candy store, was misplaced. It should come before things get too serious, before the tragedy of the second act. So we transposed it with the 'Cool' number [which makes more sense later] where the kids are starting to fall apart. Jerome Robbins told me that they had always contemplated making this switch when the show was in tryouts but the show was such a smash that they were afraid to tamper with it; they were superstitious and thought it might spoil something."

Among the actors who read for roles in West Side Story were

Peter Falk, Tom Skerritt, Bonnie Franklin, Jill St. John, Robert Redford, Joan Tewkesbury, Yvette Mimeux, Ken Berry, Frankie Avalon, Clu Gulager, Anna Maria Alberghetti, Richard Chamberlain, George Hamilton, Troy Donahue, Burt Reynolds, Joey Heatherton, Elizabeth Ashley, Gary Lockwood, George Segal, Keir Dullea, Leonard Nimoy, Jack Nicholson, Bobby Darren, Warren Beatty and Suzanne Pleshette.

Awards: Academy Awards: Best Picture [Producer: Robert Wise]; BEST DIRECTOR (Robert Wise, Jerome Robbins); Supporting Actor (George Chakiris); Supporting Actress (Rita Moreno); (Color) Cinematography (Daniel L. Fapp); Sound (Todd-AO Sound Dept. and Samuel Goldwyn Sound Dept.); Scoring of a Musical Picture (Saul Chaplin, Johnny Green, Sid Ramin, Irwin Kostal); Editing (Thomas Stanford); (Color) Costume Design (Irene Sharaff). And a special Oscar to Jerome Robbins "for his brilliant achievements in film choreography."

New York Film Critics Award: Best Picture.

Golden Globe Awards: Best Motion Picture--Musical; Supporting Actress (Rita Moreno); Supporting Actor (George Chakiris); Most Promising Newcomers (Richard Beymer; other promising newcomers were Bobby Darin, Warren Beatty, Christine Kaufmann, Ann-Margret and Jane Fonda).

The Writers Guild of America Awards: Best-Written American Musical (Ernest Lehman).

The Directors Guild of America Awards: Director Award: Robert Wise, Jerome Robbins.

The Harvard Lampoon's "Movie Worsts" Award: The Kirk Douglas Award to the Worst Actor (Richard Beymer); The Uncrossed Heart (To the least promising young actor of the year): Richard Beymer; The Worst Duos of the Year: Natalie Wood and (1) Warren Beatty, (2) Richard Beymer, (3) Anyone; The Merino Award: Rita Moreno for saving West Side Story from Natalie Wood and Richard Beymer; The Great Ceremonial Hot Dog (for the worst scenes of the cinema season): "Richard Beymer singing 'Maria' in West Side Story"; The Roscoe Award: "To Natalie Wood for so gallantly persisting in her career despite a total inability to act."

A 1977 poll by the American Film Institute named West Side

Story as one of the fifty Greatest American Films of All Time.

Reviews: "Every moment of the drama has validity and integrity, got from skillful, tasteful handling of a universal theme. Ernest Lehman's crackling screenplay, taken from Arthur Laurents' book, and Robert Wise's incisive direction are faithful and cinema-wise, and the performances are terrific..." (Bosley Crowther, The New York Times, October 19, 1961).

"Everything about West Side Story is supposed to stun you with its newness, its size, the wonders of its photography, editing, choreography, music. It's nothing so simple as a musical, it's a piece of cinematic technology." (Pauline Kael).

Wise Comments: "I've been asked many times what my favorite film is and I've had to say each time that I didn't have one favorite -- maybe six or eight. But when you put it 'artistically,' I suppose [my favorite is] West Side Story: what its challenges were, what it took to do it in the artistic sense." [A86]

"I was in New York doing post-production work on Odds Against Tomorrow when I got a call from Harold Mirisch on the Coast asking me if I would be interested in doing West Side Story. I jumped out of my seat because I had seen it two or three years before and just thought it was marvelous. It was the last few weeks of its stage run in New York, so I went to a matinee and loved it [again].

"I was to be producer and director on the film. Jerry Robbins, who directed and choreographed the stage show, had the right to do the movie choreography if he chose. Of course, I was anxious to have Jerry do [the movie] because he's such an exceptional, unusual and classic talent. But when he was approached, he declined. He said unless he could be more involved in the making of the film than just the choreography, he would rather not do it. I said jokingly to Mirisch, 'Why don't you let him direct the film?'

"Now I knew I could get one or two of his assistants to come out from New York and reproduce his choreography. But I also knew that Jerry, being the special talent that he is, would find more to do and more ways to adapt and change and do new things and creative things. So I took off my director's cap and put on the producer's cap and looked in the mirror and said, 'What's the best thing for the picture?' And the answer had to come back, 'Get Robbins on it if there's any way you can work it out.'

"It took many months of soul-searching both on Jerry's part and my part to finally come to a sort of meeting of the minds on the way that this might work [but] eventually he did come and work on the show. He co-directed about half the film with me. We were getting terribly behind schedule, way over budget and United Artists was getting increasingly nervous. Finally, the decision was made that co-directing was slowing us down too much and in order to get on with it and not to go any more over budget, we'd just have to ask Jerry to leave. Jerry was upset and I was unhappy about it but it had to be done. Fortunately for me and the film he had rehearsed all the balance of the numbers that we hadn't shot and his assistants stayed on to help me do it. But Jerry was involved in all aspects of the films from scripting to music to sets and costumes. His contribution was of such stature and such quality that I felt he definitely deserved co-directing credit with me and he got it.

"There is quite a difference in putting a musical on the screen and on the stage. In stage convention you accept people breaking into song out of dialogue, going into a dance...you're in a theatre and you accept that. It's a different situation on the screen. The screen is a very real medium; it's very difficult to get into musical things out of dialogue without feeling a little sense of awkwardness or embarrassment and that's the thing that we struggled with more than anything else: how to capture the quality of all the marvelous stylized, poetic and theatrical movements of the stage show into the realistic medium of the screen.

"One of the solutions was the opening of the film, the flight over New York. That was my idea, I wanted to show New York as a real city, because that's where our story is taking place. At the same time, by shooting straight down in the patterns and forms the city gave us, we delivered this 'real' New York in an abstract way. I think this helped [put the audience in] a frame of mind that was able to accommodate accepting the kids breaking into a dance early in the show." [A85]

Video Availability: MGM/UA Home Video (letterboxed laser disc; Wise appears in a brief prologue explaining how the laser disc was transferred from an original 65mm print). CBS/Fox Video (panned-and-scanned cassette) and The Voyager Company's Criterion Collection (letterboxed laser disc). This version contains an interview with Wise conducted by director Jeremy Kagan, storyboards, location scouting footage, casting notes, set designs, footage from the premiere, the original theatrical trailer, memos from Art Director Boris Leven, scene-by-scene analysis and other valuable and fascinating behind-the-scenes material. Wise himself assisted in the film to tape transfer.

F50   TWO FOR THE SEESAW (1962).

Seesaw Pictures. The Mirisch Company. Argyle Enterprises. Talbot Productions--Seven Arts Production. Released through United Artists.

Produced by Walter Mirisch; DIRECTED BY ROBERT WISE; Screenplay: Isobel Lennart; Based on the play by William Gibson; Director of Photography: Ted McCord; Assistant Directors: Jerome M. Siegel, John Flynn; Production Manager: Allen K. Wood; Wardrobe: Bert Henrikson, Irene Caine; Makeup: Frank Westmore; Hairstyles: Alice Monte; Music: Andre Previn; Art Director: Boris Leven; Costumes: Orry-Kelly; Editor: Stuart Gilmore; Panavision. 119 minutes.

Cast: Robert Mitchum (Jerry Ryan); Shirley MacLaine (Gittel Mosca); Edmon Ryan (Frank Taubman); Elisabeth Fraser (Sophie); Eddie Firestone (Oscar); Billy Gray (Mr. Jacoby); Ken Berry; Anne Guilbert; Oren Curtis; Sean McGregor; Barbara Slate; Sylvia Walden; Harold Gould; Larry Breitman; Malachy McCourt; John Hanek; Vic Lundin; Paul Lewis; Dwight McDonald; Bryan O'Byrne.

Reviews: "...directed...with humanity and delicacy. It is one of the year's best pictures." (James Powers, Hollywood Reporter, October 30, 1962).

Notes: In the original stage production of 1958, starring Anne Bancroft and Henry Fonda, the stage set consisted of two apartments, side by side. Wise decided to retain this basic setup for the film, using exteriors only sparingly to "give it some air."

Two For The Seesaw was originally announced to star Elizabeth Taylor and Paul Newman, to be directed by Delbert Mann. In the early 1970s, the play was revamped as a musical and renamed Seesaw; it starred Ken Howard and Michele Lee.

Awards: ACADEMY AWARD NOMINATIONS: Black-and-White

Cinematography (Ted McCord); Song--"Song From Two For The Seesaw (Second Chance)" by Andre Previn and Dory Langdon.

Video Availability: MGM/UA Home Video (both panned-and-scanned cassette and letterboxed laser disc). The laser disc contains the original theatrical trailer.

F51   THE HAUNTING (1963).

M-G-M US/British. An Argyle Enterprises Picture. A ROBERT WISE Production.

PRODUCED AND DIRECTED BY ROBERT WISE. Screenplay: Nelson Gidding; Based on the novel "The Haunting of Hill House" by Shirley Jackson; Director of Photography: Davis Boulton; Editor: Ernest Walter; Music: Humphrey Searle; Assistant Director: David Tomblin; Production Designer: Elliot Scott; Associate Producer: Denis Johnson; Special Effects: Tom Howard, F.R.P.S.; Recording Supervisor: A. W. Watkins; Camera Operator: Alan McCabe; Sound Recordist: Gerry Turner; Claire Bloom's Clothes by Mary Quant; Wardrobe Supervisor: Maude Churchill; Dubbing Editor: Allan Sones; Dubbing Mixer: J. B. Smith; Casting Director: Irene Howard; Continuity: Hazel Swift; Set Decorator: John Jarvis; Makeup: Tom Smith; Hairdresser: Joan Johnstone; Sketch Artist: Ivor Beddoes. Panavision. 112 minutes

Cast: Julie Harris (Eleanor Vance); Claire Bloom (Theodora); Richard Johnson (Dr. John Markway); Russ Tamblyn (Luke Sannerson); Lois Maxwell (Grace Markway); Fay Compton (Mrs. Sannerson); Rosalie Crutchley (Mrs. Dudley); Valentine Dyall (Mr. Dudley); Diane Clare (Carrie Fredericks); Ronald Adam (Eldridge Harper); Freda Knorr (2nd Mrs. Crain); Howard Lang (Hugh Crain); Mavis Villiers (Landlady); Verina Greenlaw (Dora); Paul Maxwell (Bud); Claude Jones (Fat Man); Susan Richards (Nurse); Amyu Dalby (Abigail at 80); Rosemary Dorken (Companion).

Reviews: "...a fearsome, harrowing, happily shivery tale of terrifying things unseen and unheard." (Cue, September 14, 1963).

"With an over-emphatic sound and music track and plenty of distorting lenses, [it is] a ponderous affair and [its] atmosphere...is due mainly to Boulton's cinematography, the special effects and excellent acting from Harris and, especially, Bloom." (Phil Hardy; B38)

Notes: The film's working title was Night Cry. Filmed in England at a manor house about ten miles outside Stratford-on-Avon. Claire Bloom's character Theo is a Lesbian, a fact merely alluded to in the film as we know it. But an early cut of the film contained a scene showing Theo leaving her female lover after a violent argument. Wise insists that the scene wasn't cut for reasons of censorship but for drama: "It seemed too much when we saw the first cut," he says. "It hit things too hard. As we viewed the film [her Lesbianism] seemed to be coming through more naturally in the course of the story, so we cut out that early sequence." [Interview with Frank Thompson, September, 1990]

The first shots of Hill House are remarkably evocative of Xanadu in Citizen Kane, though Wise denies having in mind an homage to his days with Orson Welles. The style, however, of The Haunting very directly recalls his beginnings with Val Lewton. He says, "One of the things that intrigued me about doing it was returning to my roots." [Interview with Frank Thompson, September, 1990]

Wise Comments: "While I was working on West Side Story, I read a review in Time Magazine of a book called "The Haunting of Hill House" by Shirley Jackson. It was quite an interesting review and I immediately checked to see if it had already been picked up [for motion picture production]; usually before a book is even in print the big companies have glommed onto it. But this was free so I rushed out and bought a copy and came back to my office at Goldwyn to read it. I will never forget that I was sitting there reading "The Haunting of Hill House" and in the middle of one of these very scary sequences the hair was starting to curl on the back of my neck. And [screenwriter] Nelson [Gidding] rushed through the door to ask me a question and I jumped about three feet off that couch! I said, "Oh boy, if this thing can do on the screen what it just did to me on the page, we'll have a fine classy horror picture here.

"I had the rights purchased for me and Nelson wrote a screenplay. I thought I would do it through the Mirisch Company but somewhere along the line they went kind of cool on it, there was a change of production staff, and "The Haunting of Hill House" went into turnaround. A year or two before I had been under contract to M-G-M and I had gotten angry at them and forced them to let me out of the contract before it was over. But I had agreed to give them one more picture. I was talking with my agent Phil Gersh about this and said, "Well, maybe we'll take 'The Haunting of Hill House' to M-G-M." They were interested but only if I kept it at a very modest budget, about a million dollars. I couldn't make it for that in Hollywood - the best I could do was around a million, four. But around that time I was going to London for a command performance of West Side Story. Someone suggested that the M-G-M studio in England could give us a better price. So I took a copy of the book with me, gave it to the people at the studio, gave them a copy of the script and a few weeks later they got back to me with a budget of a million, fifty. So that's how it got made in England, even though we kept the New England background; I felt that the haunted house is a little fresher in the states; they're around every corner in England.

"I thought the subject lent itself to Panavision and of course I insisted that it be filmed in black and white; I had that spelled out in my contract. This kind of film is generally a lot of fun for directors; you can do so much with sets, photography, lighting, lenses, music, sound effects. I wanted a specific look for The Haunting, and as much depth of field as I could get. The widest angle you could get in a Panavision lens was 35mm. So I called [Panavision President] Bob Gottschalk and asked him if he didn't have anything wider. He said they were working on, I think, a 28mm lens but that it still had some flaws and distorted the picture. I said, 'That's exactly what I want!' He very reluctantly sent it to me and made me sign a paper saying that I wouldn't hold him responsible for any distortion in the lens.

"Davis Boulton was a still photographer who had only done a couple of pictures as cinematographer with [director] Andrew Stone. [Production Designer] Elliot Scott was very taken with his work and convinced me to talk with him. Davis left all the handling of the camera to the operator Alan McCabe and the setups to me. He concentrated strictly on lighting with marvelous results; I was terribly pleased with his job.

"I've been asked many times about that shot going up the winding stairway in the library. We designed the railing to be like a dolly track and attached a little handheld camera to it, rigged it with wire. So we lit the scene and simply turned the camera loose so that it simply slid down to the bottom. Then we reversed the film.

"My insistence on shooting The Haunting in black and white stood me in good stead recently when they wanted to colorize it. It was spelled out in my contract that the film would be shot in black and white and that any changes or remakes or new versions could only be done with my consent. So they backed off. That's the last black and white film I made." (Interview with Frank Thompson, September, 1990)

Video Availability: MGM/UA Home Video (letterboxed laser disc). The laser disc also features the original theatrical trailer.

F52   THE SOUND OF MUSIC (1965).

20th Century-Fox. A ROBERT WISE Production. An Argyle Enterprises, Inc. Picture.

PRODUCED AND DIRECTED BY ROBERT WISE. Screenplay: Ernest Lehman; Based on the play with book by Howard Lindsay and Russel Crouse, lyrics by Oscar Hammerstein II and music by Richard Rodgers. As produced on the stage by Leland Hayward, Richard Halliday, Richard Rodgers and Oscar Hammerstein II, from the book "The Story of the Trapp Family Singers" by Maria Trapp, with the partial use of ideas by George Hurdalek. Associate Producer: Saul Chaplin; Music and additional words and music ("I Have Confidence in Me" and "Something Good"): Richard Rodgers; Lyrics: Oscar Hammerstein, II; Music Supervisor, Arranger and Conductor: Irwin Kostal; Production Designer: Boris Leven; Director of Photography: Ted McCord, A.S.C.; Choreography: Marc Breaux, Dee Dee Wood Breaux; Puppeteers: Bil and Cora Baird; Second Unit Supervision and Continuity Sketches: Maurice Zuberano; Vocal Supervision: Robert Tucker; Film Editor: William Reynolds, A.C.E.; Additional Photography: Paul Beeson; Sound: Murray Spivack, Bernard Freericks, Douglas O. Williams, Eugene Grossman; Unit Production Manager: Saul Wurtzel; Assistant Director: Ridgeway Callow; Second Assistant Director: Richard Lang; Dialogue Coach: Pamela Danova; Music Editor: Robert Mayer; Casting: Owen McLean and Lee Wallace; Set Decorations: Walter M. Scott, Ruby Levitt; Special Photographic Effects: L.B. Abbott, Emil Kosa, Jr.; Sound Recording Supervisors: Fred Hynes, James Corcoran; Makeup: Ben Nye and Bill Buell; Hair Styles: Margaret Donovan and Ray Foreman; Boom Man: Orrick Barrett; Cable Man: Jesse Long; Key Grip: Walter Fitchman; Best Boy: Fred Richter and Jack Dimmack; Gaffer: Jack Brown; Property Master: Eddie Jones; Assistant Prop Master: Benny Greenberg; Todd-AO Developers: American Optical Company and Magna Theatre Corporation; Superpanorama 70 camera: Modern Cinema System-Film; Unit Publicist: Mike Kaplan; Assistant Publicity: Carol Shapiro; Camera Operator: Paul Lockwood; Camera Technician: Roger Shearman; Assistant Art Director: Harry Kemm; Art Illustrator:

Leon Harris; Assistant Film Editor: Larry Allen; Recorder: William
Buffinger; Second Assistant Director: Richard Lang; Production
Assistant: Alan Callow; Dialogue Coach: Pamela Danova; Script
Supervisor: Betty Levin; Costume Designer: Dorothy Jeakins; Men's
Wardrobe: Richard James; Women's Wardrobe: Josephine Brown; Julie
Andrews' Makeup: Willard Buell; Hairdresser: Ray Foreman; Still
Photographer: James Mitchell; Gaffer: Jack Brown; Key Grip: Walter
Fitchman; Property Master: Ed Jones; Rehearsal Pianist: Harper
MacKay; School Teachers: Frances Klamt and Jean Seaman; Julie
Andrews' Stand-in: Larri Thomas; Charmian Carr's Stand-in: Gabriele
Henning; Re-Recording: Todd-AO and 20th Century-Fox Studios; Titles:
Pacific Title and Art Studio. Filmed in Todd-AO and Superpanorama 70
(aerial shots only). Color by Deluxe. 174 minutes.

Songs and Musical Numbers: "The Sound of Music" (Andrews);
"Praeludium" (nuns' chorus); "Morning Hymn and Alleluia" (Nuns'
chorus); "Maria" (Lee, Nixon, Baker, Nelson); "I Have Confidence in
Me" (Andrews); "Sixteen Going on Seventeen" (Carr, Truhitte); "Climb
Every Mountain" (Wood); "Lonely Goatherd" (Andrews, Baird
Marionettes); "Do-Re-Mi" (Andrews, children); "Something Good"
(Andrews, Plummer); "Edelweiss" (Plummer, Andrews, children); "So
Long, Farewell" (children); "Processional" (instrumental); "My Favorite
Things" (Andrews).

Cast: Julie Andrews (Maria Augusta Kutschera); Christopher
Plummer (Capt. Gaylord von Trapp); Eleanor Parker (Baroness Elsa
Schraeder); Richard Haydn (Max Detweiler); Peggy Wood (Mother
Abbess); Charmian Carr (Liesl von Trapp); Heather Menzies (Louisa von
Trapp); Nicholas Hammond (Friedrich von Trapp); Duane Chase (Kurt
von Trapp); Angela Cartwright (Brigitta von Trapp); Debbie Turner
(Marta von Trapp); Kym Karath (Gretl von Trapp); Anna Lee (Sister
Margaretta); Portia Nelson (Sister Berthe); Ben Wright (Herr Zeller);
Daniel Truhitte (Rolfe); Norma Varden (Frau Schmidt); Gil Stuart
(Franz); Marni Nixon (Sister Sophia); Evadne Baker (Sister Bernice);
Doris Lloyd (Baroness Ebberfeld); Maria Trapp (Ball Guest); The Bil Baird
Marionettes. Christopher Plummer's vocals: Bill Lee; Peggy Wood's
vocals: Margery MacKay.

Awards: Academy Awards: Best Picture [Producer: Robert
Wise], BEST DIRECTOR (Robert Wise), Sound, Film Editing, Scoring of
Music - Adaptation or Treatment.

Academy Award nominations: Best Actress (Julie Andrews),

Supporting Actress (Peggy Wood), Art Direction and Set Decoration, Cinematography and Costume Design.

Golden Globe Awards: Best Motion Picture - Musical/Comedy; Best Actress - Musical/Comedy (Julie Andrews).

Writers Guild of America Award: Best-Written American Musical (Ernest Lehman).

Directors Guild of America Award: BEST DIRECTOR (Robert Wise).

Producers Guild Award: David O. Selznick Award (Robert Wise).

A 1977 survey by the American Film Institute named The Sound of Music one of the fifty greatest American films of all time.

Reviews: "This last, most remunerative and least inspired, let alone sophisticated, of the Rodgers and Hammerstein collaborations is square and solid sugar. Calorie-counters, diabetics, and grown-ups from eight to eighty had best beware." (Judith Crist, The New York Herald Tribune, March 3, 1965)

"They have taken this sweet, sometimes saccharine and structurally slight story...and transformed it into close to three hours of visual and vocal brilliance." (Philip K. Scheuer, The Los Angeles Times, March 7, 1965)

"One of the top musicals to reach the screen...a warmly-pulsating, captivating drama set to the most imaginative use of the lilting [Rodgers and Hammerstein songs], magnificently mounted and with a brilliant cast." (Daily Variety, March 1, 1965)

Notes: Filmed March 26 - September 1, 1964 at 20th Century-Fox Studios and on location in Salzburg and Salzkammergut, Austria. The story of the Trapp Family had already been told on film in two West German productions: Die Trapp-Familie (1956) and its sequel Die Trapp-Familie in Amerika (1958). The two films were edited together and released in the United States by 20th Century-Fox as The Trapp Family (1961). The Sound of Music's New York premiere took place on March 2, 1965 and the Los Angeles premiere on March 10, 1965.

The Sound of Music was dubbed -- both dialogue and singing -- for foreign markets. According to a New York Times Magazine story in 1966, it was also re-named for different countries: Love and Tenderness (Egypt), Music in the Heart (Portugal), Charms of the Heaven-Sound (Thailand), Smiles and Tears (Spain), The Rebellious Novice (Argentina), My Song, My Dream (Germany), Fairy Music Blow Fragrant Place, Place Hear (Hong Kong).

According to Julia Antopol Hirsch's book The Sound of Music: The Making of America's Favorite Movie, the following actors auditioned for roles in the film: Mia Farrow, Richard Dreyfuss, Victoria Tennant, Geraldine Chaplin, Sharon Tate, Leslie Ann Warren, Patty Duke, Kurt Russell, Shelley Fabares, Teri Garr, Paul Peterson, Ann Jillian and the Osmond Brothers.

And, in assessing the popularity and impact of The Sound of Music, let us not forget Mrs. Myra Franklin of Cardiff, Wales, who saw the film 940 times.

Video Availability: CBS/Fox Video. A deluxe letterboxed laser disc, released in 1994, was transferred from a 65mm stereo print. At 176 minutes, the film takes up three sides (with audio commentary by Wise on an alternate sound track) and there are three more sides of extra material: an original production short introduced by Charmian Carr; original theatrical trailers; radio advertising and promotional interviews; an eighty-seven minute documentary From Fact to Phenomenon, which includes interviews from the cast, filmmakers and Trapp family members; and an interactive stills archive. The THX digital transfer was supervised by Wise.

F53   THE SAND PEBBLES (1966).

20th Century-Fox. Argyle-Solar Productions.

PRODUCED AND DIRECTED BY ROBERT WISE. Associate Producer/Second Unit Director: Charles Macguire; Screenplay: Robert Anderson. Based on the novel by Richard McKenna; Production Designer: Boris Leven; Director of Director of Photography: Joseph MacDonald, A.S.C.; Music: Jerry Goldsmith; Conducted by Lionel Newman; Production Associate: Maurice Zuberano; Film Editor: William Reynolds, A.C.E.; Unit Production Manager: Sol Wurtzel; Assistant Director: Ridgeway Callow; Special Effects: Jerry Endler; Sound:

Murray Spivack, Douglas O. Williams, Bernard Freericks; Second Unit Director of Photography: Richard Johnson; Set Decorations: Walter M. Scott, John Sturtevant, William Kiernan; Special Photographic Effects: L.B. Abbott, A.S.C., Emil Kosa, Jr.; Costume Designer: Renie; Location Construction Supervisor: Herbert Cheek; Wardrobe: Ed Wynigear; Technical Advisor: Harley Misiner, MMC,USN (RET.); Orchestrations: David Tamkin, Arthur Morton; Makeup: Ben Nye, Bill Turner, Del Acevedo; Hair Styles: Margaret Donovan; Diversions: Irving Schwartz. Color by DeLuxe. Panavision. Westrex Recording System. 195 minutes.

Cast: Steve McQueen (Holman); Richard Attenborough (Frenchy); Richard Crenna (Collins); Candice Bergen (Shirley); Marayat Andriane (Maily); Mako (Po-han); Larry Gates (Jameson); Charles Robinson (Ensign Bordelles); Simon Oakland (Stawski); Ford Rainey (Harris); Gavin Macleod (Crosley); Joseph di Reda (Shanahan); Joe Turkel (Bronson); Richard Loo (Major Chin); Barney Phillips (Franks); Shepherd Sanders (Perna); Gus Trikonis (Restorff); James Jeter (Farren); Tom Middleton (Jennings); Paul Chínpae (Cho-jen); Tommy Lee (Chien); Henry Wang (Lop-eye Shing); Stephen Jahn (Haythorn); Jay Allan Hopkins (Wilsey); Steve Ferry (Lamb); Ted Fish (Wellbeck); Loren James (Coleman); Glenn Wilder (Waldron); Beulah Quo (Mama Chunk); James Hong (Victor Shu).

Awards: ACADEMY AWARD NOMINATIONS: Best Picture; Best Actor (Steve McQueen); Supporting Actor (Mako); Color Cinematography (Joseph Macdonald); Color Art Direction (Boris Leven); Film Editing (William Reynolds); Original Music Score (Jerry Goldsmith).

Although The Sand Pebbles won none of the Oscars for which it was nominated, Robert Wise received The Irving G. Thalberg Memorial Award.

GOLDEN GLOBE AWARDS: Supporting Actor (Richard Attenborough); World Film Favorite--Male (Steve McQueen)

Reviews: "It is one of those none-too-frequent motion pictures which suggest that the wide screen and fast, subtle color film and stereophonic sound have not been invented in vain and are, in fact, not even luxuries but necessities for the modern filmmaker." (Charles Champlin, Los Angeles Times December 25, 1966).

Notes: The Sand Pebbles is set in the China of 1926 when warlords demanded that "treaty powers" leave Chinese soil. Much of the action takes place on the gunboat USS San Pablo, which polices the Yangste River. Wise and his crew spent six months in Taiwan and Hong Kong recreating the turbulent period. Because Taiwan was then at war, the Sand Pebbles company worked under military jurisdiction. According to 20th Century-Fox publicity, the company endured an earthquake, several storms and a hotel fire. In addition they were "interested and disturbed bystanders" during a three day riot. The Sand Pebbles was the first major American film made in Taiwan.

Publicity materials call the San Pablo the most expensive moving prop ever built. She was built in Hong Kong by Vaughn and Jung Engineering Ltd. at a cost of $200,000. The high-stacked gunboat was 150 feet long and carried a workable three-inch gun on the bow and a one-pounder cannon on the stern. Many viewers at the time saw The Sand Pebbles as a thinly-veiled allegory of America's involvement in Vietnam, so it is slightly ironic to note that, after production, the San Pablo was refitted and shipped to Vietnam to serves as a floating hotel and dormitory for American construction crews.

Wise Comments: "The Sand Pebbles has always been one of my favorite films, I suppose, because it's the most difficult film -- from a physical and logistical standpoint -- that I've ever made. I suppose having suffered through months and months and months of shooting on it, and the weather problems and everything else that went into it, makes it a more memorable experience than the others.

"If I had it to do over I suppose I would have simplified the film some. The last time I saw it I felt that maybe it would have been better off without the multiple story. Maybe we split our interests too much with the Frenchy/Maily story and would have been better off sticking with Steve [McQueen], Po-Han, the missionaries and the girl and simplifying the story." [A85]

Video Availability: CBS/Fox Video (panned-and-scanned cassette and letterboxed laser disc), Facets Multimedia (panned-and-scanned cassette).

F54   STAR! (1968).

20th Century-Fox.

Produced by Saul Chaplin. DIRECTED BY ROBERT WISE. Screenplay: William Fairchild; Based in part on "Gertrude Lawrence As Mrs. A." by Richard Aldrich; Daniel Massey's dialogue by Noel Coward; Director of Photography: Ernest Lazslo; Special Photographic Effects: L. B. Abbott, Art Cruickshank and Emil Kosa Jr.; Production Designer: Boris Leven; Set Decorations: Walter M. Scott, Howard Bristol; Editor: William Reynolds; Sound: Murray Spivack, Douglas O. Williams and Bernard Freericks; Wardrobe: Ed Wynigear, Adele Balkan; Costumes: Donald Brooks; Miss Andrews' Hairstyles: Hal Saunders; Makeup: William Buell, William Turner; Production Manager: Saul Wurtzel; Production Associate: Maurice Zuberano; Assistant Director: Ridgeway Callow; Dance and Musical Numbers Staged by Michael Kidd; Music Supervised and Conducted by Lennie Hayton; Dance Assistant: Shelah Hackett; Dance Music Composed by: Jay Thompson; Music Editor: Robert Tracy. Todd-AO. Color by Deluxe (with black and white scenes). 174 minutes.

Songs and Musical Numbers: "Star!" (Jimmy Van Heusen and Sammy Cahn); "Down At The Old Bull and Bush" (H. Von Tilzer, H. Sterling, L. Hunting and P. Krone); "Piccadilly" (Paul Morande, Walter Williams and Bruce Seiver); "Oh, It's a Lovely War" (J.P. Long, Maurice Scott); "In My Garden of Joy" (Saul Chaplin); "Forbidden Fruit," "Someday I'll Find You," "Has Anyone Seen Our Ship?" (Noel Coward); "'N' Everything" (Bud G. De Silva, Gus Kahn and Al Jolson); "Burlington Bertie From Bow" (William Hargreaves); "Parisian Pierrot" (Noel Coward); "Limehouse Blues" (Philip Brahm, Douglas Furber); "Someone To Watch Over Me," "Dear Little Boy," "Do, Do, Do" (George and Ira Gershwin); "My Ship," "Jenny" (Kurt Weill and Ira Gershwin).

Cast: Julie Andrews (Gertrude Lawrence); Michael Craig (Sir Anthony Spencer); Robert Reed (Charles Fraser); Beryl Reid (Rose); Alan Oppenheimer (Andre Charlot); Richard Crenna (Richard Aldrich); Daniel Massey (Noel Coward); Bruce Forsyth (Arthur Lawrence); John Collin (Jack Roper); Richard Karlan (David Holtzman); Lynley Laurence (Billie Carleton); Garrett Lewis (Jack Buchanan); Elizabeth St. Clair (Jeannie Banks); Jenny Agutter (Pamela Roper); Anthony Eisley (Ben Mitchell); Jock Livingston (Alexander Woolcott); J. Pat O'Malley (Dan); Harvey Jason (Bert); Damian London (Jerry Paul); Richard Angarola (Cesare); Matilda Calnan (Dorothy); Lester Matthews (Lord Chamberlain); Bernard Fox (Assistant to Lord Chamberlain); Murray Matheson (Bankruptcy Judge); Robin Hughes (Hyde Park Speaker); Anna Lee (Hostess); Don Crichton (Gertrude's Limehouse Blues Dance

Partner); Peter Church (Newsreel Narrator); Jan Gernat (Stage
Manager); Conrad Bain (Salesman at Cartier's); The Daffodil Girls:
Jeanette Landis (Eph); Dinah Ann Rogers (Molly); Barbara Sandland
(Mavis); Ellen Plasschaert (Moo); Ann Hubbell (Beryl); Josephine Gillick,
Penny Francis, Kim McCarthy, Sally Harrison (Gertie at various ages);
Max Faulkner (Corporal Cooper); Barbara Oglivie (Mary); Suzanne
France (Choreographer); Clive Morton (General); Frank Singuineau
(African Ambassador); John Woodnutt (2nd Speaker Hyde Park
Corner); Anna Turner (Mrs. Klasen); Andrew Downie (Drunken Soldier);
James Beck (Drunken Soldier); Frank Jarvis (1st Soldier at St. James'
Place); Danvers Walker (Lt. Martindale); John Barrett (Speaker at Hyde
Park); John Trevor (Noel Coward as a child); Edwin Brown, Chris
Gannon (Speakers at Hyde Park); William Mervin (General); Joan
Haythorne (Italia Conti); Robert Rietty (French Ambassador); Wesley
Murphy (Sentry); Brian Peck, Paul Harris (Soldiers); Roger Delgardo
(French Ambassador); Lynn Perry, H. E. West, Haskell Coffin (Men at
Noel's Party); Jean MacRae, Laura Mason, Ruth Warshawsky (Women
at Noel's Party); Pat Becker (Mrs. Fraser); Ted DuDomaine (English
Roue); Cicely Walper (English Woman at Noel's Party); Winnie
McCarthy, Charlott Knight (Women in Brixton Music Hall); Sean Burton
MacGregor, William O'Toole, Ian Abercrombie, Lewis Loughran, Danny
Dee (Men in Brixton Music Hall); Geoffrey Steele (Englishman at Noel's
Party); Linda Peck (Actress); Lionel Ames (Roman Officer); Yutta
D'Arcy (Vestal Virgin); Eric Brotherson (Elder Statesman); Queenie
Leonard (Grand Dame); Russ Saunders (Stuntman); Barbara Ann
Warkmeister, Joseph Casstevens, Barry Mitchell, Mel Warkmeister
(Flying Hillary's Trapeze Act); Carol Ferges, Dar Robinson, Paula Del
(Utility Acrobats); Ray Saunder (Acrobatic Act); Judy Jacobs (Web
Girl); Audrey Saunders, Ruggera Lauber (Iron Jaw Act); Charles
Charles, Lisl Charles (Wire Act); Austin Green (Ring Master); John
Ramirez, Roger Arroyo, Marilyn England, Jo Ann Norvell (Dwarfs); Dick
Wilson (Drunk); Elizabeth St. Clair (Jeannie Banks); Jan Bickmore (Web
Girl); Bob Gordon, Justus Motter, Wally Bickmore (Web Men); Darryl
Ferges (Tumbler); Monty Whitney (Call Boy "Red Peppers"); Damian
London (Jerry Paul); Eric Heath (Court Clerk); Ysabel MacCloskey,
Gerald Peters (Guests in Gertie's Dressing Room); Gwyneth Cullimore,
Alex Finlayson, Eric Mickelwood, Daphne Field, Pamela Kosh (Guests
on Bus); Pat Tidy, Wendy Atkin (Women -- Hyde Park); Stanley Fraser,
John Levingston (Men -- Hyde Park); Jack Carol (Newsreel
Cameraman); Robin Hughes (2nd Speaker at Hyde Park); Harold Ayer,
Mike Freeman (Men -- Adelphi Theatre); Merri Wood-Taylor (Woman --
Adelphi Theatre); Brenda Bennett, Gay Hartwig, Lisa Davis, Anna Lee
Austin, Catherine Allen, Jill Sanzo, Jean Christopher (Fox Chorus Girls);

Gwen Watts Jones (Mrs. Wilson); Ray Girardin (Young Reporter); Anna Lee (Hostess); Trevor Doughty (Host); Walter Reed (Photographer); Peter Ashton (Harry); Francis Napier, Philip Bailey (Singing Soldiers); Cathleen Cordell (Vendeuse); Linda Barret (Woman -- Bundles For Britain); Irene Linsley, Roy Monsell, Peter Forster (Guests -- Gertie's Dressing Room); Charles Davis (Writ Server); Richard Angarola (Cesare); Gil Stuart (Footman); Kenny Adams, Ralph Montgomery (Reporters); Steve Woodman (Man); Barry Macollum (Dan); Albert Leon (Charlot's Assistant); Danny Rees (Juggler); John Barclay (Elderly Tragedian); Bernard McDonald (Ron James); Betty Russell, Mildred Shay (Women Reporters); Jerry Fitzgerald (Harold).

Notes: Star! began filming in April, 1967. It was produced at 20th Century-Fox Studios in Los Angeles and on location in New York City (eighteen locations, in fact: The Algonquin Hotel, Music Box Theatre, Lyceum, 45th Street Theatre, among them), Cape Cod, Massachusetts (Dennis Playhouse), London (Westminster School), and France (the French Riviera, Medi Roc Villa on Cape Ferrat, the Antibes). With a cost of $14 million ($350,000 on wardrobe alone), Star! was released on November 1, 1968. After poor reviews and disastrous box-office, the film was withdrawn from release on July 1, 1968. A few months later, on October 1, 1969, it was released under the new title Those Were The Happy Times and with a new running time: 120 minutes. The re-release prints were in 35mm and mono sound only.

A brief promotional film, Star! The Sound of a Legend, was produced in 1968. It contains some voice-over narration by Julie Andrews, interesting production footage (including color shots of scenes that are only seen in black and white in the film itself), costume sketches, and numerous shots of Wise directing, Andrews working out dance numbers with choreographer Michael Kidd, and other behind-the-scenes footage.

The credits for this film are: Executive Producer: Ronald Saland; Director: Elliot Geisinger; Photographer: Marcel Broekman; Writer: Jay Anson; Editor: Hortense Beveridge.

Awards: Star! received Academy Award nominations for Supporting Actor (Daniel Massey); Cinematography; Art Direction/Set Decoration; Sound (20th Century-Fox Sound Dept.); Musical Score; Song ("Star!" music by Jimmy Van Heusen and lyrics by Sammy Cahn); Costume Design.

Daniel Massey received a Golden Globe as Best Supporting Actor.

The Harvard Lampoon's "Movie Worst" Awards named Star! as one of the year's Ten Worst Movies.

Notes: Critically bashed in 1968, in retrospect, Star! seems quite a brave film, utilizing a complex flashback technique in which an older Gertrude Lawrence watches a newsreel review of her life [more shades of Citizen Kane]. The film continually jumps from a black and white, 1.33 to 1 aspect ratio to the brilliant color and wide screen of Todd-AO, with some sequences beginning in one and continuing in the other. Braver still is the idea of placing a charismatic, but basically unsympathetic, character at the center of a brassy, glitzy musical; that it is sweet Julie Andrews who is playing this complex woman, makes Star! seem even more remarkable.

Wise Comments: "The critical response to Star! really disappointed me. But it played recently [1990] in New York City and it went over like gangbusters. The audience applauded after every number and gave me and the film such a hand. I think it's a very underrated film and Julie is just extraordinary in it; it's very sophisticated.

"I often wondered if the poor response had to do with the public's unwillingness to accept Julie as the kind of character that Gertrude Lawrence was, a lady who can get drunk and high, who's slept around a bit, that sort of thing. In real life she's no goody-goody. She's a real lady with an aura of quality about her but she can appreciate a dirty joke and whatnot. Every time she's tried to do something a little more dramatic and heavy it hasn't worked out well commercially for her." (Interview with Frank Thompson, September, 1990).

Video Availability: CBS/Fox Home Video. A deluxe letterboxed laser disc, released in 1994, contains much supplementary material including behind-the-scenes footage and interviews with Wise and Julie Andrews.

F55   THE SERGEANT (1968).

Warner Bros. -- Seven Arts. A ROBERT WISE Production.

EXECUTIVE PRODUCER: ROBERT WISE. Producer: Richard Goldstone; Director: John Flynn; Screenplay: Dennis Murphy. Based upon his novel, "The Sergeant"; Director of Photography: Henri Persin; Production Designer: Willy Holt; Supervising Film Editor: Charles Nelson, A.C.E.; Film Editor: Francoise Diot; Art Director: Mark Frederix; Music: Michel Magne; Production Manager: Serge Lebeau; Technical Advisor: Donald Roth; Camera Operator: Gilles Bonneau; Sound: Julien Coutellier; Makeup: Michel Deruelle; Dialogue Coach: Elliott Sullivan; Continuity: Alice Ziller; Assistant Director: Louis Pitzele; Publicist: Al Hix. Technicolor. MPAA Rating: R. 107 minutes.

Cast: Rod Steiger (the Sergeant); John Phillip Law (Swanson); Ludmila Mikael (Solange); Frank Latimore (Captain Loring); Elliott Sullivan (Pop Henneken); Ronald Rubin (Corporal Cowley); Philip Roye (Aldous Brown); Jerry Brouer (Sergeant Komski); Memphis Slim (Night Club Singer).

Notes: The homosexual theme of The Sergeant made the film slightly notorious upon original release. According to publicity, the army post set was the largest ever built in France, covering twenty-five acres. Built at Stuios de Boulogne, near Paris, the sets were devised so that scenes could easily change simply by reversing the camera angle.

F56 THE BABY MAKER (1970).

A ROBERT WISE Production.

EXECUTIVE PRODUCER: ROBERT WISE; Producer: Richard Goldstone; Director and Screenwriter: James Bridges; Music: Fred Karlin; Cinematographer: Charles Rosher Jr.; Film Editor: Walter Thompson; Art Director: Mort Rabinowitz; Sound: Larry Jost; Unit Production Manager: Herb Willis; Assistant Directors: Howard W. Koch Jr. and Joseph M. Ellis; Dialogue Coach: Geoffrey Horne; Script Supervisor: Michael Preece; Camera Operator: Robert Byrne; First Assistant Cameraman: Matthew F. Leonetti; Second Assistant Cameraman: Ken Hale; Still Photographer: Floyd McCarty; Set Decorator: Raymond Paul; Property Master: Ted Cooper; Makeup Artist: Wesley Dawn; Hair Stylist: Maryce J. Bates; Ladies' Costumer: Jean Merrick; Men's Costumer: Robert B. Richards; Gaffer: Patrick R. Blymer; Key Grip: Lawrence E. Milton; Best Boy: Gary Holt; Generator Operator: Harry Getz; Grip: John Vusich; Boom: Clint Althaus; Cable: Sale Robinson; Props: Ted Cooper and Art Lipschultz; Lead Man:

Charles Gay; Special Effects: Thol O. Simonson; Assistant Film Editor: John Hanley; Greensman: Phil Michaels; Driver Captain: Joe R. Sawyers; Sketch Artist: William B. Major; Production Secretary: Myrtle Von Stein; Director's Secretary: Elian W. Harris; Transportation: Frenchie De Rosher, Bob Conte, John Mulder, August Hilder, Bill Cockrell, Bob Benton, Bob Elsey, Arne Pohjola, A. Bucklinger, Frank Auston, Joe Marks. MPAA Rating: R. 109 minutes.

Cast: Barbara Hershey (Tish Gray); Collin Wilcox-Horne (Suzanne Wilcox); Sam Groom (Jay Wilcox); Scott Glenn (Tad Jacks); Jeannie Berlin (Charlotte); Lili Valenty (Mrs. Culnick); Helena Kallianiotes (Helena); Robert Pickett (Dr. Sims); Paul Linke (Sam); Phyllis Coates (Tish's Mother); Madge Kennedy (Tish's Grandmother); Ray Hemphill (George); Brenda Sykes (Frances); Michael Geoffrey Horne (Jimmy); Jeff Siggins (Stoned Young Man); Charlie Wagenheim (Toy Shop Owner); Bob Ennis (Exotica); Mimi Doyle (Woman Clerk); Patty Dietz (Nurse); Pat Hedruck (Lamaze Prepared Childbirth Instructress); and Jonathan Green, Michael Scroggins, Samuel Francis, Allen Keesling, Charles Lippincott, Peter Mays, Jeffrey Perkins (The Single Wing Turquoise Bird Light Show).

Video Availability: Warner Home Video Inc.

F57   THE ANDROMEDA STRAIN (1971).

Universal.

PRODUCED AND DIRECTED BY ROBERT WISE. Screenplay: Nelson Gidding; From the novel by J. Michael Crichton; Production Designer: Boris Leven; Director of Photography: Richard H. Kline, A.S.C.; Unit Production Manager: Ernest B. Wehmeyer; Art Director: William Tuntke; Set Decorations: Ruby Levitt; Sound: Waldon O. Watson, James Alexander, Ronald Pierce; Music: Gil Melle; Film Editors: Stuart Gilmore, John W. Holmes, A.C.E.; Special Photographic Effects: Douglas Trumbull, James Shourt; Costumes: Helen Colvig; Matte Supervisor: Albert Whitlock; Production Illustrator: Thomas Wright; Music Engineering: Allan Sohl; Makeup: Bud Westmore; Hair Stylist: Larry Germain; Script Supervisor: Marie Kenney; Technical Advisors: Dr. Richard Green, George Hobby, William Koselka; Titles and Optical Effects: Universal Title/Attila De Lado; Assistant Director: Ridgeway Callow. Scientific Background Support by Cal Tech and the Jet Propulsion Laboratory. Animal Sequences Filmed Under the

Supervision of the American Humane Association and M. W. Blackmore, D.V.M. Scientific Equipment from Perkin-Elmer Corp., Central Research Labs, Inc., R.C.A., Concord Electronics Corp., Du Pont Instrument Products Division, Van Waters and Rogers, Technicon Corp., and Honeywell Corp. MPAA Rating: G. Panavision. Technicolor. 131 minutes.

Cast: Arthur Hill (Dr. Jeremy Stone); David Wayne (Dr. Charles Dutton); James Olson (Dr. Mark Hall); Kate Reid (Dr. Ruth Leavitt); Paula Kelly (Karen Anson); George Mitchell (Jackson); Ramon Bieri (Major Manchek); Kermit Murdock (Dr. Robertson); Richard O'Brien (Grimes); Peter Hobbs (General Sparks); Eric Christmas (Senator From Vermont); Mark Jenkins (Lt. Shawn); Peter Helm (Sgt. Crane); Ken Swofford (Toby); Richard O'Brien (Grimes); Michael Pataki (Mic T); John Carter (Capt. Morton); Carl Reindel (Lt. Comroe); Joe DiReda (Burke); Richard Bull (Air Force Major); David Mclean (Senator from New Mexico); Frances Reid (Mrs. Dutton); Susan Brown (Allison Stone); Bart LaRue (Medic Captain); James W. Gavin (Dempsey, Helicoptor Pilot); Michael Bow (M.P. Sergeant); Walter Brooke (Secretary of Defense); Reuben Singer (Dr. Karp); Garry Walberg (Technician); Ivor Barry (Murray); Midori (Lab Assistant); Glenn Langan (Secretary of State); Paul Ballantyne (Hospital Director); Len Wayland (Officer, Jet Crash Site); Dr. Harold O. Dyrenforth (Irving Schwartz); George Schmidt (Old Lady - Piedmont); Quinn Redeker (Capt. Morris); Judy Farrell (Pam); Joan Swift (Uniformed Girl); Dee Carroll, Sandy DeBruin (Girl Technicians); Emory Parnell (Old Doughboy); Jan Burrell (Mother); Duke Cigrang (Father); Jason Johnson (Dr. Benedict); Francisco Ortega (Gateman at Agricultural Station); Tom McDonough (Stetson); Johnny Lee (Boy); Gary Waynesmith, Rob Hughes (Air Force Technicians); Cliff Medaugh, Russ Whiteman (Civilians); William Dunbar (Air Force Sergeant); Joe Billings, Ray Harris, Ted Lehmann (Scientists); Lisa Daniels, Lorna Thayer, Alma Platt (Ad Lib Women); Lance Fuller, Gil Stuart (Ad Lib Men); Shiela Guthrie (Girl); Jamie Lamb (Boy); Clark Savage (M.P. Sergeant); Colin G. Male, H.E. West, Glenn Dixon (Senators); David E. Frank (Gunner Wilson); Ben Pfeiffer (Pilot); Bob Olen (Soldier); Carl B. Morrison (Man); Rhodie Cogan (Woman); Donald T. Ellis (Man); Patty Bodeen, Sandy Ego (Young Girls); Victoria Meyerink (Little Girl); Paul Stader (Stuntman).

Awards: The Andromeda Strain received Academy Award nominations for Art Direction (Boris Leven, William Tuntke, Ruby Levitt) and Film Editing (Stuart Gilmore, John W. Holmes).

The Harvard Lampoon's "Movie Worsts" Awards skewered The Andromeda Strain twice: "The Piltdown Mandible (to the most obviously and unabashedly spurious scientific phenomenon); and "The Ayn Rand Award" (to that writer whose bad books made even worse movies) to Michael Crichton.

Reviews: "Wise's direction, immensely aided by superb special photographic effects by Douglas Trumbull and James Shourt, and an overall production design by Boris Leven, is especially clean and economic, and in many ways, The Andromeda Strain is his best film in years." (Larry Cohen, Hollywood Reporter, March 10, 1971).

Video Availability: MCA/Universal Home Video (letterboxed laser disc). The laser disc also features the original theatrical trailer in which Wise appears onscreen.

F58   TWO PEOPLE (1973).

Universal. A Universal-Filmakers Group Picture.

PRODUCED AND DIRECTED BY ROBERT WISE. Screenplay: Richard De Roy; Director of Photography: Henri Decae; New York Sequences Photographed by Gerald Hirschfeld A.S.C.; Camera Operator: Yves Rodallac; Music: David Shire; Editor: William Reynolds A.C.E.; Art Director: Harold Michelson; Set Decorations: Eric Simon; Sound: Antoine Petitjean, Waldon O. Watson, Ronald Pierce; Titles and Optical Effects: Universal Title; Wardrobe Mistress: Tanine Autre; Miss Wagner's Wardrobe: Holly Harp; Makeup: Monique Archambault; Hairstyles: Alex Archambault; Production Managers: Ridgeway Callow (U.S.) and Enrico Isacco (France); Production Assistants: Jon Bloom and Latif Lahlou; Property Master: Daniel Braunschweig; Assistant Directors: Denis Amar and Larbi Bennani (Morocco); Assistant and Interpreter: Mohamed Abbazi. MPAA rating: R. Technicolor. 101 minutes.

Cast: Peter Fonda (Evan Bonner); Lindsay Wagner (Deidre McCluskey); Estelle Parsons (Barbara Newman); Alan Fudge (Fitzgerald); Philippe March (Gilles); Frances Sternhagen (Mrs. McCluskey); Brian Lima (Marcus McCluskey); Geoffrey Horne (Ron Kesselman).

Reviews: "Director Wise has made some excellent movies...but has become better known of late for such otiose blockbusters as <u>The Sound of Music</u> and <u>Star!</u>, <u>Two People</u> looks to be his attempt to get to a smaller, more meaningful scale, but he seems to be still out of touch with the most basic kind of emotional reality." (Jay Cocks, <u>Time</u>, April 2, 1973).

Notes: <u>Two People</u> was filmed on location in Marrakech, Casablanca, Paris and New York. Originally scheduled to be a Filmmakers Group production from Columbia Pictures, "irreconcilable differences" between Wise and the studio resulted in a move to Universal in December, 1971.

Wise began scouting locations in Morocco in October, 1972. The crew arrived there on January 23, 1973 and began film exactly one month later. Wise used a unionized French crew and brought in equipment from Paris and the Soussi studio in Rabat.

F57   <u>THE HINDENBURG</u> (1975).

Universal/Filmakers Group. A ROBERT WISE Production.

DIRECTED BY ROBERT WISE. Screenplay: Nelson Gidding; Screen Story: Richard Levinson, William Link; Based on the Book by Michael M. Mooney; Director of Photography: Robert Surtees, A.S.C.; Production Designer: Edward Carfagno; Film Editor: Donn Cambern; Special Visual Effects: Albert Whitlock; Costumes: Dorothy Jeakins; Music: David Shire; Special Photography: Clifford Stine, A.S.C.; Set Decorations: Frank McKelvey; Sound: Leonard Peterson, Don Sharpless, John A. Bolger, John Mack; Sound Effects: Peter Berkos; Special Mechanical Effects: Glen Robinson, Andrew Evans, Frank Brendel, Robert Beck; Continuity Illustrator: Thomas Wright; Technical Advisor: George Lewis; Unit Production Manager: Ernest Wehmeyer; 1st Assistant Director: Howard Kazanjian; 2nd Assistant Director: Wayne Farlow; Stunt Coordinator: John Daheim; Matte Photography: William Taylor; Makeup: Del Acevedo, Frank McCoy, Rick Sharp; Hair Styles: Lorraine Roberson; Men's Wardrobe: Tony Scarano; Assistant Film Editor: Todd Ramsay; Sound Effects Editor: Peter Berkos; Still Photographer: Larry Barbier; Titles and Optical Effects: Universal Title. Panavision. Technicolor. MPAA Rating: PG. 120 minutes (125 minutes in television network debut).

Song: "There's A Lot To Be Said For The Fuhrer" Music by

David Shire, Lyrics by Edward Kleban. Performed by Robert Clary and Peter Donat.

Cast: George C. Scott (Ritter); Anne Bancroft (The Countess); William Atherton (Boerth); Roy Thinnes (Martin Vogel); Gig Young (Edward Douglas); Burgess Meredith (Emilio Pajetta); Charles Durning (Captain Pruss); Richard A. Dysart (Lehmann); Robert Clary (Joe Spah); Rene Auberjonois (Major Napier); Peter Donat (Reed Channing); Alan Oppenheimer (Albert Brestau); Katherine Helmond (Mrs. Mildred Breslau); Joanna Moore (Mrs. Channing); Stephen Elliott (Captain Fellows); Joyce Davis (Eleanore Ritter); Jean Rasey (Valerie Breslau); Ted Gehring (Knorr); Lisa Pera (Freda Halle); Joe di Reda (Schulz); Peter Canon (Ludecke); Charles Macauley (Kirsch); Rex Holman (Dimmier); Jan Merlin (Speck); Betsy Jones-Moreland (Stewardess Imhoff); Colby Chester (Eliot Howell III); Teno Pollick (Frankel); Curt Lowens (Elevator Man Felber); Kip Niven (Lt. Truscott); Michael Richardson (Rigger Neuhaus); Herbert Nelson (Dr. Eckener); Scott Walker (Gestapo Major); Ruth Kobart (Hattie); Greg Mullavey (Morrison); Val Bisoglio (Lt. Lombardi); Simon Scott (Lutwaffe General); William Sylvester (Luftwaffe Colonel); David Mauro (Goebbels); Joseph Turkel (Detective Moore); Sandy Ward (Detective Grunberger); Johnny Lee (Paul Breslau); Stephen Manley (Peter Breslau); Rolfe Sedan (Luther).

Awards: The Hindenburg was nominated for Academy Awards for Cinematography (Robert Surtees); Art Direction-Set Decoration (Edward Carfagno, Frank McKelvy); Sound (Leonard Peterson, John A. Bolger, Jr., John Mack, Don K. Sharpless).

The Hindenburg received "Special Achievement" Oscars for Sound Effects (Peter Berkos) and Visual Effects (Albert Whitlock, Glen Robinson).

Reviews: "Technically the film is a triumph; dramaturgically, it is somewhat less than that. Its climax is terrifyingly, horrendously spectacular, but the two hours getting there are not as gripping as they might have been." (Kevin Thomas, Los Angeles Times, December 21, 1975).

Notes: At 7:25 p.m. on May 6, 1937, the zeppelin Hindenburg arrived at Lakehurst, New Jersey after a flight from Frankfurt, Germany. As the airship approached its mooring dock, it burst into flames, then exploded, killing fifteen passengers, twenty crewmen and one line handler. After an inquest, the official cause of the disaster was listed as "St. Elmo's Fire." However, the Gestapo had believed that a bomb was placed aboard The Hindenburg and Col. Fritz Erdmann, Maj. Franz Hugo and Lt. Klaus Hinkelbein came along as passengers to keep an eye on things.

Michael Mooney's book "The Hindenburg" takes the position that the disaster was, indeed, an act of sabotage and Nelson Gidding's script agrees. The bomb on board Wise's Hindenburg is put there by a young radical (William Atherton) protesting the growing list of atrocities by Hitler's government.

The real Hindenburg was over 800 feet long containing a total of 7,200,000 cubic feet of explosive hydrogen gas. It was capable of a speed of eighty knots and carried enough fuel for a 10,000 mile flight. There were cabins for seventy passengers, a special smoking room (with one electric lighter; no open flames were allowed anywhere else on the ship), a dining room, a library, three bars, a lounge and a promenade deck with slanting windows.

When Wise was approached by Universal in 1973 he was concerned with the challenge of bringing this doomed zeppelin to life on the screen. He met with Visual Effects artist Albert Whitlock who assured Wise that, with a combination of matte paintings, models and other sophisticated special effects techniques, The Hindenburg could indeed fly once more. A scale replica of the ship, twenty-five feet long, was built for the long shots. It had working lights, four simulated Diesel engines and a remote-control motor; it would even dump water ballast.

Parts of the ship would, of course, have to be constructed at full size. The nose cone, belly and fin, and catwalk areas of The Hindenburg were built on Stage 12 at Universal Studios. The sets used eight tons of aluminum, 11,000 yards of muslin, 24,000 feet of sash cord and two million rivets.

In researching the film Wise and Art Director Edward Carfagno visited the Smithsonian Institute and the National Archives in Washington, D.C., archives in Berlin, the Deutsche Museum in Munich, and the small manufacturing town of Friedrichschafen where a lighter-than-air museum held actual pieces of The Hindenburg. Wise also met the son of The Hindenburg's last Captain who supplied the company with important photographs and color postcards of the interior of the ship.

Many films -- including The Wizard of Oz and Butch Cassidy and the Sundance Kid -- begin in black and white and then blossom to full color for the main body of the picture. But The Hindenburg is in color throughout -- until the last reel. Wise believed that, no matter how skillfully done, Hollywood special effects could never match the raw horror of the actual newsreel footage (taken by three cameras) of the disaster. He decided to make those final scenes a mixture of real and recreated footage. "...we came up with the idea of just letting the explosion blow the color off the screen," Wise wrote [A73]. "As it is now, the explosion goes to white, filling the screen. Then we come back to black and white and stay that way until the very tag." However, because Universal wanted protection, in case Wise's stylized climax didn't work, the fire footage was also filmed in color.

Although the actual Hindenburg disaster took only 34 seconds, the sequence in the film runs to about six minutes.

The Hindenburg began filming on August 12, 1974. Scenes were filmed in Munich (doubling for pre-war Frankfurt), Milwaukee, New York City, Washington, D.C. and El Toro Marine Base in Santa Ana, California which doubled for Lakehurst, New Jersey. The explosion was filmed on Stage 12 at Universal. Because of the intense flames involved in this sequence, a large venting hole was cut in the roof of the stage. The twisted skeleton of the post-crash Hindenburg was placed on the tarmac of the El Toro Marine Base.

Albert Whitlock created seventy matte paintings that, combined with the model and live-action footage, convincingly portrayed the grace and power of The Hindenburg in flight. For one sequence, in which the airship passes over Amsterdam, Whitlock's crew faced an interesting problem. Whitlock wrote, "Obviously, what was called for was some three-dimensional method of showing the millions of lights of the city moving by below -- but how to do that without some sort of very expensive and time-consuming construction? What started out as a big problem was solved by a neophyte assistant who suddenly said, 'How about doing it with sugar granules -- the kind that confectioners use?' And, by golly, that's what we did in the end. A table was built with a winch that could move it past the camera. The table was covered with black velvet and the whole thing was sprinkled with the kind of confections you put on Christmas trees -- little globules of sugar of different colors. They were pushed around with the straight edge of a ruler to arrange them in patterns that looked very much like those of streetlights you see from an airplane -- or, in this case, a zeppelin." [A72]

Video Availability: MCA/Universal Home Video (letterboxed laser disc). The laser disc also features the original theatrical trailer.

F58   AUDREY ROSE (1977).

United Artists. A ROBERT WISE Production.

Produced by Joe Wizan and Frank De Felitta. DIRECTED BY ROBERT WISE. Screenplay: Frank De Felitta, based upon his novel; Director of Photography: Victor J. Kemper, A.S.C.; Music Composed and Conducted by: Michael Small; Editor: Carl Kress; Casting: Lynn Stalmaster; Production Manager: Charles H.Maguire; Costumes: Dorothy Jeakins; Production Designer: Maurice Zuberano; Sound: Tom Overton, William McCaughey, C.A.S., Aaron Rochin, C.A.S., Michael J. Kohut; Special Effects: Henry Millar, Jr.; 1st Assistant Director: Art Levinson; 2nd Assistant Director: Leslie Moulton; Camera Operator: Bob Thomas; Script Supervisor: Marie Kenney; Assistant Art Director: George Szeptycki; Makeup: Frank Griffin; Hairdresser: Jean Austin; Women's Costumer: Shirlee Strahm; Men's Costumer: Sheldon Levine; Property Master: Marty Wunderlich; Orchestrations: Jack Hayes; Music Editor: Milton Lustig; Construction Coordinator: Bob Krume; Head Electrician: Dick Hart; Key Grip: Bob Rose; Consultation on Hypnosis: Jean Holroyd, Ph.D.; Court Technical Advisor: Daniel A. Lipsig; Assistant to the Producers: Betty Gumm; Production Co-ordinator: Rosalyn Catania; Still Photographer: Wynn Hammer. Production Services by Rock Company/Persky-Bright. Lab processing by Metro-Goldwyn-Mayer; Release Prints by Deluxe General; Panavision. MPAA Rating: PG. 113 minutes.

Cast: Marsha Mason (Janice Templeton); Anthony Hopkins (Elliot Hoover); John Beck (Bill Templeton); Susan Swift (Ivy Templeton); Norman Lloyd (Dr. Steven Lipscomb); John Hillerman (Scott Velie); Robert Walden (Brice Mack); Philip Sterling (Judge Langley); Ivy Jones (Mary Lou Sides); Stephen Pearlman (Russ Rothman); Aly Wassil (Maharishi Gupta Pradesh); Mary Jackson (Mother Veronica); Richard Lawson (Policeman #1); Tony Brande (Detective Fallon); Elizabeth Farley (Carole Rothman); Ruth Manning (Customer in Store); Stanley Brock (Cashier in Store); David Wilson (Policeman #2); David Fresco (Dominick); Pat Corley (Dr. Webster); Eunice Christopher (Mrs. Carbone); Karen Anders (Maria, Waitress).

Reviews: "Lest The Sound of Music and West Side Story...obscure the fact, one must remember that Robert Wise's long career embraces many films of low-key, environmental suspense and terror and fear...it is no surprise that Audrey Rose is Wise's best film in some years." (Variety, April 6, 1977).

"Not since The Haunting has Robert Wise had such a grand opportunity to suggest that there are worlds beyond the realm of our five senses. [Here] he makes at least one of those worlds so palpable that it might even be true." (Arthur Knight, Hollywood Reporter, April 6, 1977).

"Solidly craft by Wise and mercifully free of special effects trickery...a surprisingly watchable film if one can ignore the handicap of a script steeped in transcendental banality." (Phil Hardy; B38)

Notes: Director Joan Darling was brought onto the production to assist Susan Swift, making her acting debut, with her performance.

Wise Comments: "On Audrey Rose we had one scene, a big argument scene between John Beck and Marsha Mason, which we had rehearsed, but when it came to filming that scene, it somehow didn't feel right. Frank [De Felitta, the scriptwriter and co-producer] said, 'Why don't we let John and Marsha just go at it. They're aware of where they are in the story and they know the characters.' They did and really got at each other. We had a tape recorder there and Frank went back to work and took dialog out of that. We shaped it a bit and the scene in the film is based on their improvisation. It's a much better scene than it was in the script - one of the strongest in the picture. I like to give the actors their head once we've agreed early on about the character they're playing, the story, the plot, the whole body of the film. Mine is a prepared approach with ample room for improvising as we go along." [A132]

Video Availability: MGM/UA Home Video

F61 STAR TREK -- THE MOTION PICTURE (1979).

Paramount.

Produced by Gene Roddenberry; DIRECTED BY ROBERT WISE; Screenplay: Harold Livingston; Story: Alan Dean Foster; Music: Jerry

Goldsmith; Based on the television series "Star Trek," created by Gene Roddenberry; Director of Photography: Richard H. Kline, A.S.C.; Production Designer: Harold Michelson; Editor: Todd Ramsay; Special Photographic Effects Directed by: Douglas Trumbull; Special Photographic Effects Supervised by: John Dykstra; Special Photographic Effects Produced by: Richard Yuricich; Executive in Charge of Production: Lindsley Parson, Jr.; Associate Producer: Jon Povill; Special Animation Effects: Robert Swarthe; Special Science Supervisor: Jesco Von Puttkamer; Special Science Consultant: Isaac Asimov; Costume Designer: Bob Fletcher; Set Decorator: Linda DeScenna; Makeup Artists: Fred Phillips, Janna Phillips, Ve Neill; Hair Stylist: Barbara Minster; Sound Mixer: Tom Overton; Music Editor: Ken Hall; Unit Production Manager: Phil Rawlins; Assistant Director: Danny McCauley; Second Assistant Director: Doug Wise; Art Direction: Joe Jennings, Leon Harris, John Vallone; Prop Master: Dick Rubin; Script Supervisor: Bonnie Prendergast; Assistant Film Editors: Rick Mitchell, Randy D. Thornton; Supervising Sound Editor: Richard L. Anderson; Sound Editors: Stephen Hunter Flick, Cecelia Hall, Alan Murray, Colin Waddy, George Watters II; Sound Effects Created by: Dirk Dalton, Joel Goldsmith, Alan S. Howarth, Francisco Lupica, Frank Serafine; Dialogue Editor: Sean Hanley; Supervising Re-Recording Mixer: Bill Varney; Re-Recording Mixers: Steve Maslow, Gregg Landaker; Construction Coordinator: Gene Kelley; Mechanical Special Effects: Alex Weldon, Darrell Pritchett, Ray Mattey, Marty Bresin; Graphics: Lee Cole; Production Illustrators: Maurice Zuberano, Michael Minor; Publicity: John Rothwell, Suzanne Gordon; Still Photographer: Mel Traxel; DGA Trainee: Kevin Gremin; Accountant: Charles A. Ogle; Secretary: Anita Terrian; Camera Operator: Al Bettcher; Assistant Cameramen: Michael Genne, Rob Wise; Gaffer: Larry Howard; Key Grip: Bob Sorbel; Wardrobe: Agnes Henry, Jack Bear; Special Assistant to Mr. Roddenberry: Susan Sackett; Special Photographic Effects: Dave Stewart; Director of Photography: Richard Yuricich; Matte Paintings: Matthew Uricich; Additional Matte Paintings: Rocco Gioffre; Miniatures: Greg Jein, Russ Simpson, Jim Dow; Special Photographic Effects: Don Baker; Cameramen: Phil Barbiero, Don Cox, Douglas Bey, John Ellis, David Hardberger, Alan Harding, Don Jarel, Lin Law, Clay Marsh, David McCue, Max Morgan, Scott Squires, Hoyt Yeatman; Additional Photography: Jim Dickson, Bruce Logan; Special Photographic Effects Editorial: Jack Hinkle, Vicki Witt; Special Electronic and Mechanical Design: Evans Wetmore, Richard Hollander; Production Illustrators: David Negron, Andy Probert, Tom Cranham, Robert McCall, Don Moore; Special Mechanical Design: George Polkinghorne; Special Visual Consultants: Virgil Mirano, Guy Marsden; Special Photographic Effects

Gaffer: David Gold; Special Photographic Effects Grip: Pat Van Auken; Special Effects Props and Miniatures: Larry Albright, Bruce Bishop, Al Broussard, Chris Crump, Lee Ettleman, Mike Fink, Kris Gregg, Rick Guttierez, Mike McMillen, Tom Pahk, Chris Ross, Robert Short, Robert Spurlock, Mark Stetson, Rick Thompson, Paul Turner, Don Wheeler; Special Photographic Effects Director of Photography: Thane Berti, Glenn Campbell, Christopher George, Scott Farrar, Robert Friedstand, Robert Hollister, Russ McElhatton, Mike Peed, Lex Rawlins, Jonathon Seay, Steve Slocum, Bob Thomas; Animation and Graphics: Deena Burkett, Alison Yerka, Lisze Bechtold, Merllyn Ching, Elrene Cowan, Cy Didjurgis, Leslie Ekker, Linda Harris, Nicola Kaftan, John Kimball, Thomas Koester, Deidre Le Blanc, Linda Moreau, Connie Morgan, Paul Olsen, Greg Wilzbach; Special Electronics: Kris Dean, Stephen Fog, John Gilman, Jim Goodnight, Fred Iguchi, Robin Leyden, Greg McMurray, Mike Myers, Josh Morton; Special Editorial: Michael Backauskas, Kathy Campbell, Nora Jeanne Smith; Special Photographic Effects Projectionist: John Piner; Special Photographic Effects Project Managers: John James, Bill Millar; Special Assistants to Photographic Effects: Leora Glass, Brett Webster; Special Optical Consultants: Alan Gundelfinger, Milt Laiken; Special Mechanical Designs: George Randle Co., Precision Machine, Dieter Seifert, Rourke Engineering; Transportation Coordinator: Robert Mayne; Special Photographic Effects Sequences: Apogee, Inc.; Special Photographic Effects Supervised by: John Dykstra; Special Photographic Effects Project Manager: Robert Shepherd; Special Photographic Effects Cameramen: Chuck Barbee, Bruno George, Michael Lawler, Jerry Pooler, Doug Smith, John Sullivan; Miniatures Supervised by: Grant McCune; Director of Optical Photography: Roger Dorney; Special Animation Effects: Harry Moreau; Special Electronic Design: Alvah J. Miller, Matt Beck, Paul Johnson, Steve Sass; Production Illustrators: Martin Kline, Syd Meade, Jack Johnson, John Shourt; Special Mechanical Design: Dick Alexander, Bill Shourt, Don Trumbull; Special Photographic Effects Director of Photography: Cosmos Bolger, Dennis Dorney, Robert Elswitt, Phil Gonzales, Greg Kimble, Ron Nathan, Michael Sweeney, Diane E. Wooten; Special Effects Props and Miniatures: David Beasley, John Erland, Joe Garlington, Pete Gerard, Rick Gilligan, Richie Helmer, Michael Joyce, Deborah Kendall, Don Kurtz, Pat McClung, Gary Rhodaback, John Ramsay, Dennis Schultz, David Scott, Dick Singleton, Richard Smiley, David Sosalla, Susan Turner, Don Webber, Gary Weeks; Special Photographic Effects Grips: Mark Cane, Mark Kline; Special Photographic Effects Gaffer: Chuck Embrey; Wardrobe: Mary Etta Lang; Animation and Graphics: Angela Diamos, John Millerburg;

Special Photographic Effects Editorial: Denny Kelly, David Bartholomew, Steve Klein, Steve Mark; Special Visual Consultants: Mike Middleton, Erik Nash, Phil Joanou; Assistant to Mr. Dykstra: Mimi McKinney; Assistant to Mr. Shepherd: Ann M. Johnston; Special Assistance to Photographic Effects: Deborah Baxter, Janet Dykstra, Philip Golden, Proctor Jones, Tut Shortleff; Special Optical and Mechanical Consultants: B/G Engineering, Abbot Grafton, Gerald Nash; Geometric Designs: Ron Resch, Boston University; Certain Models Manufactured by Magicam, Inc.; Titles: Richard Foy/Communication Arts, Inc.; Orchestrations: Arthur Morton; Scoring Mixer: John Neal; Theme From Star Trek Television Series by Gene Roddenberry and Alexander Courage; Computer Motion Control System For Miniatures: Bo Gehring; Certain Special Visual Effects Conceived and Designed by Robert Abel and Associates, Inc.; RA and A Designs by Richard Taylor; Medical Computer Displays Courtesy of Digital Equipment Corporation; Production Kinetic Lighting Effects In Engine Room and V'Ger 6 Complex by Sam Nicholson and Brian Longbotham; Technical Assistance by Polaroid Corporation; Certain Computer Equipment by Sutherland Computer Corporation; Casting: Marvin Paige; Technical Assistants: Sayra Hummel, Junero Jennings; Stunts: Robert Bralver, William Couch, Keith L. Jensen, John Hugh McKnight. Panavision, Dolby Stereo and Metrocolor. MPAA Rating: G. 132 minutes. (An additional 12 minutes were added to network television showings and to some of the video editions, both on cassette and laser disc. However, the letterboxed laser disc is, at Wise's insistence, the length of the original theatrical version.)

Cast: William Shatner (Captain Kirk); Leonard Nimoy (Spock); DeForest Kelley (Dr. McCoy); James Doohan (Scotty); George Takei (Sulu); Majel Barrett (Dr. Chapel); Walter Koenig (Chekov); Nichelle Nichols (Uhuru); Persis Khambatta (Ilia); Stephen Collins (Decker); Mark Lenard (Klingon Captain); Billy Van Zandt (Alien Boy); Grace Lee Whitney (Janice Rand); Roger Aaron Brown (Epsilon Technician); Gary Faga (Airlock Technician); David Gautreaux (Commander Branch); John D. Gowans (Assistant to Rand);Howard Itzkowitz (Cargo Deck Ensign); Jon Rashad Kamal (Lt. Commander Sonak); Marcy Lafferty (Chief DiFalco); Jeri McBride (Technician); Michele Ameen Billy (Lieutenant); Terrence O'Connor (Chief Ross); Michael Rougas (Lieutenant Cleary); Susan J. Sullivan (Woman); Ralph Brannen, Ralph Byers, Paula Crist, Iva Lane, Franklyn Seales, Momo Yashima (Crew Members); Jimmie Booth, Joel Kramer, Bill McTosh, Dave Moordigian, Tom Morga, Tony Rocco, Joel Schultz, Craig Thomas (Klingon Crewmen); Edna Glover, Norman Stuart, Paul Weber (Vulcan Masters); Leslie C. Howard

(Yeoman).

Awards: Star Trek -- The Motion Picture was nominated for Academy Awards for Art Direction-Set Decoration; Musical Score; and Visual Effects.

Notes: The first of (at this writing) six feature films based on Gene Roddenberry's television series Star Trek which ran on NBC from 1966-69. According to Paramount publicity materials, the engine room of the Starship Enterprise stood two and a half stories tall and additional sets filled ten sound stages. Among these sets were a San Francisco tram station of the 23rd Century, an orbital dry dock, a Federation monitor station in space and the interior of a Klingon cruiser.

Reviews: "...state of the art screen magic. The expert hand of director Wise is evident in the rising suspenseful tempo and the deft blending of performances." [Variety December 12, 1979]

"...the special effects have overwhelmed the meager plot and sketchy characters. As a piece of kinetically abstract art, Star Trek is unusually pleasing to the eye. The narrative, however, is something else again." [Andrew Sarris, The Village Voice December 17, 1979]

Video Availability: Paramount Home Video (cassette and both panned-and-scanned and letterboxed laser disc).

F60   ROOFTOPS (1989).

Koch-Mark/Jett/New Visions.

Produced by Howard Koch, Jr. DIRECTED BY ROBERT WISE. Screenplay: Terence Brennan; Story: Allan Goldstein and Tony Mark; Director of Photography: Theo Van de Sande; Editor: William Reynolds; Music: David M. Stewart and Michael Kamen; Production Designer: Jeannine Claudia Oppewall; Art Director: John Wright Stevens; Set Decorator: Gretchen Rau; Special Effects: Candy Flanigan and Steve Kirshoff; Costumes: Kathleen Detoro; Choreography: Jelon Viera; Stunts: Gary Baxley; Makeup: Anne Pattison. Color by Deluxe. MPAA rating: R. 98 minutes.

Songs: "Avenue D" by David A. Stewart, Etta James, Richard Feldman, performed by Stewart and James; "Drop" by George

Chandler, Jimmy Chambers, Jimmy Helms, Liam Hensall, performed by London Beat; "Freedom" written and performed by Pat Seymour; "Rooftops" by David A. Stewart, Pat Seymour, Richard Feldman, performed by Jeffrey Osborne; "Keep Runnin" by Robert Reed, James Avery, performed by Trouble Funk; "Loving Number One" by Vince Hudson, Jude Hudson, performed by Kisses From the Kremlin; "Revenge (Part II)" by David A. Stewart, Annie Lennox, performed by Eurhythmics; "Stretch" by Charlie Wilson, David A. Stewart, performed by Wilson; "Meltdown" by David A. Stewart, Michael Kamen, performed by Joniece Jamison; "Bullet Proof Heart" by Grace Jones, Chris Stanley, performed by Grace Jones.

Cast: Jason Gedrick (T); Troy Beyer (Elana); Eddie Velez (Lobo); Alexis Cruz (Squeak); Tisha Campbell (Amber); Allen Payne (Kadim); Steve Love (Jackie-Sky); Rafael Baez (Raphael); Jaime Tirelli (Rivera); Luis Guzman (Martinez); Millie Tirelli (Squeak's mom); Robert La Sardo (Blade); Jay M. Boryea (Willie); Rockets Redglare (Carlos); Edouard De Soto (Angelo); John Canada Terrell (Jumkie Cop); Bruce Smolanoff (Bones); Edythe Jason (Lois); Paul Herman (Jimmy); Lauren Tom (Audrey); Stuart Rudin (Wino); Robert Weil (Hotel Clerk); Coley Wallace (Lester); Jose Ynoa (Young Cook); Danny O'Shea (Rookie Narc); Herb Kerr III (Jorge); Kurt Lott (Zit); Peter Lopez (Burn); Jed James (X); Woodrow Asai (Yard Foreman); Angelo Florio (Cop at Dance); Diane Lozada (Older Sister); Imani Parks (Young Sister).

Reviews: "Perhaps [Wise] saw [Rooftops] as an academic challenge. In The Haunting he set out to achieve maximum horror without ever showing anything explicit on the screen. Perhaps he viewed this new project as a similar conjuring act - trying to give the illusion of life without story, without characters, with nothing but stock elements from other films." (Andy Klein, Los Angeles Herald-Examiner, March 20, 1989).

Notes: Wise's last film as director, to date, is a return to the turf of West Side Story, filmed on location in New York City. It was also the first release from New Visions Pictures and CEO Taylor Hackford said that this was the reason they asked Wise to direct. "What is to us a lot of money may not be to a major studio. It's a great responsibility, and I wanted somebody who had a lot of experience and knew what he was doing...The film is a musical. it has dance; it's a tough urban drama; it has to have a lot of heart. And when you look around for directors who can cover that gamut, you're not going to find a very long list."

Video Availability: International Video Entertainment (cassette and laser disc).

F63 WISDOM (1986)

20th Century-Fox/Gladden Entertainment

EXECUTIVE PRODUCER: ROBERT WISE; Produced by Bernard Williams; Written and Directed by Emilio Estevez; Editor: Michael Kahn A.C.E.; Director of Photography: Adam Greenberg; Production Designer: Dennis Gassner; Music: Danny Elfman; Casting: Penny Perry; Unit Production Manager: Carl Olsen; First Assistant Director: Bernard Williams; Second Assistant Director: Donald Eaton; Stunt Coordinator: Bud Davis; Special Effects Coordinator: Richard Helmer; Art Director: Dins Danielsen; Fashion Design: Jonathon Kinsey; 2nd Second Assistant Director: Wendy Ikeguchi; Script Supervisor: Valerie Norman-Williams; Location Managers: Cass Martin, Amy Ness; Production Coordinators: Karen Dawneagle, Pamela Killebrew; Assistant to Mr. Estevez: Barbara Stordahl; Assistant to Ms. Moore: Mickey McDermott; Assistant Art Director: Nancy Haigh; Set Decorator: Richard Hoover; Assistant Set Decorator: Robin Peyton; Assistant Set Dresser: Lisa Ziegler; Lead Man: Barry Franenberg; Visual Concepts: Mentor Huebner; First Assistant Camera: Vance Piper; Second Assistant Camera: Nick Infield; Second Camera Operator: Bernard Auroux; Second Camera First Assistant: David Rudd; Additional Photography: Barry Sonnenfeld; Still Photography: Michael Paris; Sound Recordist: Ed White; Boom Operator: Matthew McFadden; Assistant Editor: Craig Bassett; Assistant Editor: Robert Frazen; Apprentice Editor: Gary Simon; Supervising Sound Editor: Andrew G. Patterson, M.P.S.E.; Sound Editors: Lucy Coldsnow, Michael J. Benavente, Mary Andrews, Michael H. Ford, Joey Ippolito; Assistant Sound Editors: Laja Holland, Cynthia Thornton; Music Editor: Bob Badami; Music Arrangements and Programming: Steve Bartek; ADR Mixers: Bob Deschaine, Linda Corbin; Voice Casting: Barbara Harris; Foley Artists: Joan Rowe, Jerry Trent; Re-Recording Mixers: Richard Portman, Thomas Gerard; Video Assistant: Edward Palacios; Casting Assistants: Megan Branman, Mae Williams; Extra Casting (L.A.): Atmosphere Agency; Extra Casting (Sacramento): Mary Dangerfield; Production Accountant: Priscilla Chelson; Assistant Accountant: Erin Jackman; Accounting Assistant: Susan Stern; Accounting Services: Zeiderman, Oberman and Associates Inc.; Wardrobe Supervisor: Nancy Cone; Costumer's Assistant: Laura Goldsmith; Chief Makeup: Kyle Tucy; Chief

Hairdresser: Tammy Kusian; Mr. Estevez's Hair Designed by Joe Torrenueva; Construction Coordinator: Frank Vivano; Property Master: Douglas Fox; Assistant Props: Russell Bobbitt, Daniel Peterson; Key Grip: Doug Wood; Best Boy Grip: Michael G. Uva; Grips: Brad Wood, Keith Tally, Bela Steven Lechoczki, Robert Studenny, Jose Santiago, Willy Nemeth; Gaffer: Jono Kouzouyan; Best Boy Electrician: Jack Yanekian; Electricians: John Pierce, Mike Molnar, Azusa Ono; Special Effects Assistants: James Schwalm, David Simmons, James Hart; Fitness Trainer: Jackson Sousa; Transportation Coordinator: Sam Edelman; Transportation Captain: Gaston "Gus" Veilleux; Unit Publicist: Marsha Robertson; Public Relations Coordinator: Andrea Jaffe; Production Assistants: Dana Williams, Matt Robinson, David Rothenberg; Craft Service: Paul Kopeikin; Stand-In for Mr. Estevez: Mark Chilingar; Stand-In for Ms. Moore: Erika Lincoln; Technical Advisor: Gil Parra; Negative Editor: Jack Hooper; Opticals by Howard A. Anderson Co.; Post Production Facilities Furnished by Lion's Gate Studios; Titles Designed by Howard A. Anderson Co.; Color by DELUXE; Camera and Lenses Provided by Otto Nemenz International, Inc.; Public Relations Representation: Rogers and Cowan (U.S. and Canada), Dennis Davidson Associates (International); Insurance Provided by Albert G. Ruben; Catering by The Arrangement, Inc., Wynt Williams, Tony Marchesi; Completion Bond by The Completion Bond Company, Inc.; Dolby Stereo. 109 minutes.

Songs: "Home Again" Performed by Oingo Boingo; "Whiskey In My Beer" Written and performed by Gary Austin; "Moonbright Misty Night" Written by Ron Gertz, Performed by Scott Wojahn; "Tears Run Down" and "Rock Me Baby" Written, performed and produced by Danny Elfman.

Cast: Demi Moore (Karen Simmons); Emilio Estevez (John Wisdom); Tom Skerritt (Lloyd Wisdom); Veronica Cartwright (Samantha Wisdom); William Allen Young (Williamson); Richard Minchenberg (Cooper); Ernie Brown (Motel Manager); Bill Henderson (Thoo); Gene Ross (Sheriff); Liam Sullivan (Jake Perry); Charlie Sheen (City Burger Manager); Hal Fishman (Network Anchor); Chuck Henry (Local Anchorman); Nick Shields (Gun Salesman); Barbara Stamm (Loan Officer at Bank #1); Santos Morales (Al Gomez); Gus Corrado (Yuppie Employer); Golden Henning (Katie); Rene Sprattling (Carol); Kate McKinnon (Nancy); Tim Sapunor (Matt); Charlie Holliday (Bob); Ron Presson (Guard at Bank #1); Estee Chandler (Female Teller); Jeff Boudov (Minnesota Bank Teller); Thomas Witt-Ellis (Albuquerque Officer #1); David DeFrancesca (Albuquerque Officer #2); Leon Corcos

(Leon); Janet Rotblatt (Elderly Lady on Street); Erika Lincoln (Woman on Street); Sid Conrad (Farmer); Henry Proach (Old Man on Street); Matt Robinson (Young Man); Bob Devon Jones (Teacher) Jimmy Walker Lane (Night Manager at Mini-Mart); Walter Edward Smith (Bank Customer #1); John Dederick (Bank Customer #2); Beau Dare (FBI Agent); Gil Parra (Swat Team Leader); Jamie Namson (Helicopter Pilot).

Stunts: Bud Davis, Eddie Braun, Hal Burton, Gary Davis, Corey Eubanks, Glory Fioramonti, Beau Gibson, Michael Hayned, Thomas Huff, Julius La Flore, Gary McLarty, Don Pike, Bernie Pock, Dennis Scott.

Reviews: "Wisdom marks 23 year-old actor Emilio Estevez' directorial debut -- and it shows. Filmmaker's naivete is evident in his completely implausible script and unending sophomoric dialog that even the young star's winsomeness can't make bearable." (Variety, December 31, 1986).

Notes: As Executive Producer, Wise was on the set every day, supervising the directorial debut of Emilio Estevez. It has been claimed that Wise eventually took over the direction when Estevez was unable to attend both to his performance onscreen and his directing chores. Wise, however, strenuously denies this. "I was always on the set, lending whatever support I could, giving advice and so forth," he said, "but I did not direct a single scene in that film. I tried to be very careful so as not to even give the impression that I was anything other than a supervising producer. Emilio directed that film, absolutely, by himself." [Interview with Frank Thompson, March 9, 1994]

Video Availability: Warner Home Video.

Bibliography

Articles

A1   Eng, Frank. "Column." <u>Los Angeles Daily News</u> (September 13, 1948).

         On Wise's career and production of <u>The Set-Up</u>.

A2   Wise, Robert. "Case History of a Crime Film." <u>Los Angeles Daily News</u> (May 8, 1952).

         On the production of <u>Captive City</u>.

A3   Nason, Richard. "Evaluating the 'Odds': Harry Belafonte Tries Broad Racial Approach in Locally Made Feature." The <u>New York Times</u> (March 15, 1959).

         Concerning Belafonte's production <u>Odds Against Tomorrow</u>, directed by Wise.

A4   Becker, Bill. "Hollywood Steps: Director Robbins' Dance Rehearsals Whip 'West Side Story' Into Shape." <u>The New York Times</u> (July 3, 1960).

A5   "20th to Film R&H's <u>Sound of Music</u>; Pays Million for
            15-Year Lease on Hit." <u>Variety</u> (June 13, 1960).

A6   Archer, Eugene. "Wise 'Story' Direction." <u>The New
            York Times</u> (October 15, 1961).

            On the production of <u>West Side Story</u>.

A7   Flynn, Hazel. "It's a Wise Man in Oscar Derby."
            <u>Citizen-News</u> (January 30, 1962).

A8   Schumach, Murray. "Hollywood 'Seesaw': Two-
            Character Hit Play Expanded For Screen." <u>The
            New York Times</u> (March 11, 1962.

            On "opening up" <u>Two For The Seesaw</u> from stage
            to screen.

A9   Schumach, Murray. "Hollywood Sweep: Oscar Triumphs
            of <u>West Side Story</u> Seen As Victory For Independents."
            <u>New York Times</u> (April 15, 1962).

A10   Stark, Samuel. "Robert Wise." <u>Films in Review</u>
            (January, 1963).

            Biographical overview.

A11   "River Come To My Door." <u>Variety</u> (August 28, 1963).

            Wise scouts locations for <u>The Sand Pebbles</u>.

A12   "Wise Helms <u>Sound</u> at 20th" <u>Variety</u> (November 5,
            1963).

A13   "Wise Words On How Gals Can Get Into Films."
            <u>Variety</u> (February 28, 1964).

            Addressing the women of the Hollywood Studio Club,
            Wise answered questions from the audience. When
            asked about what "specific qualities" he seeks in an
            actress, Wise answered, "No special qualities; simply
            someone who fits the part...Reserve is usually a good
            thing. If a girl comes on too strong, too professional -

watch out. I would advise against her."

A14   Fessier, Jr., Michael. "Director Robert Wise to Actresses: Doubt Tricky Routes For Success." (Weekly Variety March 4, 1964).

        Q and A with the women of the Hollywood Studio Club.

A15   Wise, Robert. "Why The Sound of Music Sounds Differently." Los Angeles Times Calender (January 24, 1965).

A16   Weiler, A.H. "Pebbles In the Far East." The New York Times (February 7, 1965).

        On production of The Sand Pebbles.

A17   "Theatres Sloppy on Technicalities, Sound of Music Will Check All." Variety (February 10, 1965).

A18   Cohn, Al. "He Makes Film Songbursts Believable." Newsday (March 1, 1965).

        On The Sound of Music.

A19   Scheuer, Philip K. "Sound of Music Without the Taste of Saccharine." Los Angeles Times Calender (March 7, 1965).

A20   McCord, Ted. "The Sound of Music." American Cinematographer (April, 1965).

        The production of The Sound of Music.

A21   "Gertie Lawrence Tale Long in Preparation For June 1966 Start." Variety (June 2, 1965).

        On pre-production of Star!

A22   Hopper, Hedda. "'Bobbsey Twins' Due on Screen." Los Angeles Times (October 14, 1965).

        The syndicated columnists reveals Wise's plans to make

a motion picture and television series of author Laura Lee Hope's "Bobbsey Twins" books. See "Unrealized Projects" below.

A23   Scheuer, Philip K. "Robert Wise Honored by Guild as Producer of the Year." (Los Angeles Times March 8, 1966).

The Screen Producers Guild gave Wise the award for The Sound of Music at its 14th annual Milestones Awards Dinner. Julie Andrews accepted the award for Wise, who was then on location for The Sand Pebbles.

A24   "Hong Kong Red Chinese Rag Attacks Bob Wise." (Variety May 2, 1966).

During the filming of The Sand Pebbles a Chinese newspaper, Tai Kung Pao, called Wise "an imperialist American provacateur" whose film is "anti-Communist."

A25   Kafka, John. "Munich (Hitler's Hotbed) Slashes 20th's Music, Eliminating Nazis As Heavies." Variety (June 1, 1966).

On the German "editing" of The Sound of Music which consisted of ending the movie after Maria and Baron von Trapp are married. Their escape from the Nazis was cut out entirely.

A26   "Wise Hits 'High-Handed' 20th Staffer Who Slashed Nazi Footage From Music." Variety (June 2, 1966).

A27   "Wise, Shocked by Munich's Nazi Cuts, Questions 'Power' of Branch Offices." Variety (June 8, 1966).

A28   Scheuer, Philip K. "Gunboat To Fire Wise's Next Salvo." Los Angeles Times (June 14, 1966).

On The Sand Pebbles.

A29   Weiler, A.H. "A Spy In The House of Love." New York Times (October 23, 1966).

Wise purchases Anais Nin novel of the same name.

A30   Barthel, Joan. "Biggest Money-Making Movie Of All Time - How Come?" The New York Times (November 20, 1966).

A major feature story on the making and marketing of The Sound of Music.

A31   Bart, Peter. "McQueen: 'Blue Chip' Stock." The New York Times (December 4, 1966).

Personality piece on Steve McQueen, concentrating on The Sand Pebbles.

A32   Shearer, Lloyd. "The Biggest Box Office Draw of All Time." Parade (December 18, 1966) pp.4-5.

On The Sound of Music. Wise and Julie Andrews on magazine cover.

A33   Thompson, Howard. "Candice of California: On An International Kick." The New York Times (December 18, 1966).

Personality profile of Candice Bergen who had recently completed filming The Sand Pebbles. Bergen says of Wise, "[Bob is] one of the kindest men in the world, a gentleman. Working with Bob convinced me that you should go into a picture, choosing your director, almost like a marriage. That same compatibility. It's that important."

A34   Champlin, Charles. "Brainstorms Pay Off For Hollywood's Wise Man." Los Angeles Times (December 25, 1966).

On The Sand Pebbles.

A35   "Robert Wise Hailed by His Fellow Hoosiers." Variety (March 5, 1967).

The director was feted on the occasion of the

Indianapolis premiere of The Sand Pebbles. Indiana Governor Roger D. Branigin named March 2, 1967 "Robert Wise Day" and made him a Sagamore of the Wabash.

A36   Stack, Dennis. "Film: Views and Interviews." (column) Kansas City Star (March 12, 1967).

Wise on The Sand Pebbles and career.

A37   "The Return of Robert E. Wise." The Indianapolis Star Magazine (April 2, 1967).

Written on the occasion of Wise's return to his native Indiana for the premiere of The Sand Pebbles.

A38   "Robert Wise Set For The Thalberg Award." (The Film Daily April 5, 1967).

News item regarding the upcoming Academy Award Ceremony at which Wise would be honored.

A39   Handsaker, Gale. "Film Perfectionist -- No Details Missed by Robert Wise." Newark Evening News (April 15, 1967).

Career piece upon Wise's winning of the Academy's Irving Thalberg award.

A40   Cook, Joan. "Fade In On Donald Brooks, Backstage Star." The New York Times (May 22, 1967).

Profile of the costume designer for Star!.

A41   Arneel, Gene. "Bob Wise Mentors Pix Tyros." (The Film Daily May 31, 1967).

Wise discusses his "responsibility to advise and train and teach young filmmakers."

A42   Zeitlin, David I. "Wise...The Man and His Movies." The CinemaEditor Vol. 17, #2, (Summer, 1967) pp. 11-12.

Career overview.

A43   Marlowe, Patricia. "Robert Wise." The Canyon Crier
           (September 21, 1967).

           Career article.

A44   Graham, Sheila. "The Sound of Music Is Money." New
           York Post (February 12, 1968) p. 27.

           On Wise's financial success upon completion of Star!.

A45   Klein, Doris. "Bob Wise Makes Pics For People, Not
           Himself or Other Filmmakers." Hollywood Reporter
           (April 29, 1968).

           On Star!.

A46   Beaupre, Lee. "Wise Fears Roadshow Glut." Variety
           (October 30, 1968).

           On the filming and marketing of Star!.

A47   Williams, Whitney. "Salzburg Snubs The Sound of
           Music, But Basks in the Bonanza of Tourist Booty
           Lensing of 20th-Fox Film Brought to Tow." Variety
           (June 20, 1969).

A48   Roderick, Rudolph. "Robert Wise and His Films."
           Entertainment World (December 30, 1969).

           Career article. "The important thing to me is to get as
           large an audience as I can," Wise says. "Not just for the
           commercial reasons. Those are very important,
           obviously, because if we don't pay for our negatives we
           don't keep on making films. But even more so, if you
           have some message or a theme that you feel is
           important, that you feel audiences should get, it's only
           as good as the number of people that see it."

A49   Christy, George. "Mae West Raps." Cosmopolitan (May,
           1970).

The veteran sex symbol discusses, among other subjects, her work with Wise on an unproduced television special, "A Night With Mae West."

A50   Knight, Arthur. "Wise in Hollywood." Saturday Review (August 8, 1970) pp.22-25.

           On production of The Andromeda Strain.

A51   Ornstein, Bill. "Bob Wise Says Prefers to Make His Pictures in U.S." Hollywood Reporter (December 3, 1970).

A52   Dietz, Lawrence. "Robert Wise: Man in the Middle of Film Extremes." Los Angeles Times "Calender" (April 11, 1971).

           Career article concentrating on The Andromeda Strain.

A53   Gittleson, Natalie. "Robert Wise: Mythmaker." Harper's Bazaar (May, 1971).

A54   Pickard, Roy. "The Future...a Slight Return." Films and Filming (July, 1971) pp. 27-31.

           Career overview.

A55   Wise, Robert. "Impressions of Russia." Action (July/August, 1971).

A56   "Robert Wise at Summer Seminar." American Film "A.F.I. Report" (October, 1971).

           Career article.

A57   Nogueira, Rui. "Robert Wise at RKO." Focus On Film #12, (Winter, 1972) pp.43-50.

           Wise interview and filmography. The first of three parts.

A58   "Super Pro: Dialogue With Robert Wise." Hollywood Reporter (November, 1975).

Career interview.

A59   Nogueira, Rui. "Robert Wise at Fox" <u>Focus On Film</u> #14, (Spring, 1973) pp.47-50.

Second of three-part Wise interview and filmography.

A60   Champlin, Charles. "<u>Sound of Music</u> - Hills Are Alive Again." <u>Los Angeles Times</u> (March 14, 1973).

A61   Nogueira, Rui and Eyles, Allan. "Robert Wise to Date." <u>Focus On Film</u> #16, (Autumn, 1973) pp.49-55.

Third of three-part Wise interview and filmography.

A62   "Newsmaker: Robert Wise." <u>Action</u> Volume 9, Number 2 (March-April, 1974).

A transcription of Wise's appearance on the television program <u>Newsmakers</u> (KNXT-TV, Los Angeles) in which he discussed Guild's repsonse to the recent Supreme Court decision on obscenity. Wise told interviewers Ruth Ashton Taylor, David Sheehan and Georges Fischer that the National Board of the Guild had recently passed a motion supporting a First Amendment or freedom of choice stand on the decision, "thinking of it as an infringement on our civil rights for us not to be able as consenting adults to see the kind of films we want to see."

A63   Champlin, Charles. "Robert Wise: From Cat People Curses To Fat Film Purses." <u>Los Angeles Times "Calender"</u> (September 29, 1974).

Career overview.

A64   Taylor, Douglas. "Wise Views Rising Trend of Director-Producer Role." <u>Hollywood Reporter</u> (February 3, 1975).

A65   Wise, Robert. "Butchering." <u>The New York Times</u> (February 9, 1975).

A letter protesting the editing for length of motion pictures on television.

A66   "Director Robert Wise at the 10th Chicago International Film Festival." American Cinematographer (January, 1975).

A67   Stamelman, Peter. "Robert Wise and The Hindenburg." Millimeter (November, 1975).

A68   "Dialogue On Film: Robert Wise." American Film (November, 1975).

An career interview.

Career interview.

A69   Biegel, Jerry. "Robert Wise: The Hindenburg." Action (November/December, 1975)

Article/interview in which Wise discusses the complex, sometimes frustrating process of bringing the effects-laden Hindenburg to the screen.

A70   Taylor, Nora. "The Hindenburg--a New Spy Film." Christian Science Monitor. (December 29, 1975) p. 20.

Interview with Wise.

A71   "Behind the Scenes of The Hindenburg." American Cinematographer (January, 1976).

A72   Surtees, Robert. "Photographing The Hindenburg." (American Cinematographer January, 1976).

An interview with the film's Director of Photography.

A73   Whitlock, Albert. "Reincarnating an 800-Foot Giant Superstar." (American Cinematographer January, 1976).

A74   Wise, Robert. "The Production of The Hindenburg." (American Cinematographer January, 1976).

A75   Rubin, Steve. "Retrospect: The Day The Earth Stood

Still." Cinefantastique Volume 4, Number 4 (Winter, 1976).

Admirably thorough story of how the science fiction classic was brought to the screen.

A76   "Wise is Launching 'Most Challenging'." Reba and Bonnie Reporting (column) Beverly Hills Independent (April 29, 1976).

On Audrey Rose.

A77   "Robert Wise Talks About the 'New Hollywood'." American Cinematographer (July, 1976).

A78   McBride, Joseph. "Pic Industry Has Self to Blame For Censorship Rise, says Wise." (Daily Variety July 14, 1976).

McBride quotes Wise: "We've been bringing [censorship] on ourselves. We've been overdoing the violence, at least not treating the violence as an obscenity."

A79   Reilly, Sue. "Good Actor Mix Most Important: Wise." Hollywood Reporter (September 16, 1976).

Wise discusses working with actors, stressing his recent production Audrey Rose.

A80   "Dearth of Young Writers Alarming to Robert Wise." Box Office (November 29, 1976).

A81   Lindsey, Robert. "Even Good Films Don't Know When To Stop." The New York Times (February 29, 1977).

An article on the gradual lengthening of movies. Wise is quoted comparing the average 90 minute length of films when he started directing in the 1940s to the two and a half hour films of 1977. He approves of the added length: "It allows you to develop more detail and more difficult stories."

A82   Harmetz, Aljean. "The Producer Who Didn't Want Robert Redford...He Wanted John Beck. John Beck?" New York Times (March 2, 1977).

Article about several emerging stars, including <u>Audrey Rose</u>'s John Beck.

A83   "Robert Wise: 'As The Editor, You're The Audience.'" <u>Film Comment</u> (March-April, 1977).

Wise is featured in a special 24 page section "The Film Editor." An interview concentrates on his editing of <u>Citizen Kane</u>, particularly the famous "breakfast scene." "We played with that for a long time," Wise says, "and it was in the cutting room where it was finally worked out the way it got in the picture. The rhythm of that whole...sequence was established in the cutting room, not the concept, but the rhythm..."

He also discusses the editors he, as a director, prefers to work with: William Reynolds, Stuart Gilmore, Don Cambern and others. The interview includes a list of the films Wise edited.

Elsewhere in the issue, 100 editors where asked to choose the finest editors and the directors who consistently have outstanding editing in their films. Wise appeared in the Top Ten of both lists, receiving six votes as Editor and twelve votes as a director who consistently has good editing.

A84   Appelbaum, Ralph. "<u>Audrey Rose</u> in Search of a Soul: Robert Wise Interviewed." <u>Films and Filming</u> (November, 1977).

A85   Amoruso, Marino and Gallagher, John. "Robert Wise: Part One 'The RKO Years.'" <u>Grand Illusions</u> (Winter, 1977).

Excellent interview which covers Wise's career as an editor with William Dieterle, Dorothy Arzner and others and his own directorial career through <u>The Set-Up</u>. <u>Note</u>: Although Marino Amoruso is credited as co-author of this article, he did not conduct the interviews; they were done by John Gallagher alone. Many of the quotes in the body of this bio-bibliography which are attributed to this interview actually come from the unedited transcripts of Gallagher's interviews with Wise from 1977, 1983 and 1984.

A86   Rabourdin, D. "Robert Wise." Cinema (Paris) #229
           (January, 1978) pp. 31-35.

           Career interview.

A87   Rose, Christine. "From Russia - With Connections." Los
           Angeles Times (March 2, 1978).

           Article concerning Soviet filmmakers who arrived in
           Hollywood seeking Wise's help in getting a toe-hold in
           the film industry.

A88   Keenan, Richard. "Fight Films Go To Court: The Set-
           Up/Champion Controversy." American Classic Screen
           Volume 2, Number 6 (July/August, 1978).

           Interesting article about the lawsuit which RKO brought
           against Stanley Kramer's Screen Plays II Corporation
           claiming that "Champion clearly infringes a material part
           of The Set-Up." The suit was eventually resolved after
           a Judge ordered Champion cut by 103 feet and six
           frames, shortening the original running time by one
           minute, nine seconds.

A89   Welsh, James M. "Knockout in Paradise City: an
           Appraisal of The Set-Up (1948)." American Classic
           Screen Volume 2, Number 6 (July/August, 1978).

           An analytical essay on Wise's classic boxing film.
           Author Welsh writes that The Set-Up's "greatest impact
           lies in the director's genius for creating atmosphere and
           his sensitivity of nuance and gesture."

A90   Austin, Bruce. "An Interview With Robert Wise."
           Literature/Film Quarterly, Volume VI, Number 4 (Fall,
           1978).

A91   Stein, M.L. "At Last, All Systems Are 'Go' For Star
           Trek" The New York Times (January 21, 1979).

           Feature story discussing Star Trek - The Motion Picture
           and its transformation from failed television series to
           big-budget motion picture. Story mentions, among other

interesting facts, that Wise replaced Philip Kaufman as director. Kaufman moved directly to his remake of Invasion of the Body Snatchers (1978).

A92   "Time and Again: Robert Wise." Monthly Film Bulletin (November, 1979) p. 244.

Career interview.

A93   Jones, Preston Neal. "Robert Wise" Cinefantastique Vol. 9, #2, (Winter, 1979).

Interview concentrating on Star Trek - The Motion Picture.

A94   Welsh, Jim. "Movie/Video Expo's Tribute to Robert Wise." American Classic Screen Volume 5, Number 5 (1980).

A brief, appreciative biographical essay on the occasion of Wise's being awarded The National Film Society's "Achievement in Cinema" award.

A95   "Interview re Star Trek." L'Ecran Fantastique #13 (1980) pp. 49-52.

A96   Houston, David. "Director Robert Wise Talks About The Changes and Challenges of Star Trek - The Motion Picture." Starlog (January, 1980) pp. 16-21.

A97   Guerif, F. "Nous avons gagne ce soir." Avant Scene du Cinema (March 1, 1980)

A98   "Bio-filmographie de Robert Wise." L'Avant Scene Cinema #243 (March, 1980).

A99   Schwartz, Howard. "An A.F.I. Seminar With Robert Wise and Milton Krasner, A.S.C." American Cinematographer (March, 1980).

A100   Tsao, L. G. "Rumbo a lo desconcido" Cine (Mexico; June/July, 1980).

Interview.

A101   Tedesco, Sam. "Film Editor to Oscar-Winning Director:
              Robert Wise." On The Set Volume 2, Number 4 (July,
              1980).

              Brief article/interview that concentrates on Wise's work
              as an editor at RKO. He disputes the notion that an
              editor-turned-director will shoot less film, saying that he
              shoots more film and more angles because "you know
              how valuable that extra footage will be later when the
              company's disbanded and the actors are gone."

A102   Appelbaum, R. "Techniques of the Horror Film: Or a
              Decline of Technique?" Filmmakers Monthly
              (September, 1980).

              Interview.

A103   Rubin, Steven Jay. "Sound of Music Kids - Where Are
              They Now?" Los Angeles Times Calender (April 26,
              1981).

A104   Piton, J. P. "Lexique des realisateurs de films
              fantastiques americains (5)." Image et son (September,
              1981).

A105   Keenan, Dr. Richard. "Star Trek: The (First) Motion
              Picture." American Classic Screen Volume 6, Number
              3 (1982).

              The author's journal of nearly a month spent on the set
              of Star Trek. A sidebar concerns production designer
              Maurice Zuberano and features many of his storyboard
              sketches.

A106   Bodeen, DeWitt. "Boris Karloff: An Affectionate Memoir
              of the Gentleman of Terror." American Classic Screen
              Volume 7, Number 2 (March/April, 1983).

              Bodeen, a former screenwriter for producer Val Lewton,
              profile's Karloff's contribution to Lewton's RKO
              productions, including Wise's The Body Snatcher.

A107   Wise, Robert and Menell, Jeff. "Direct It: Tips From Robert Wise." <u>Video Review</u> (June, 1983).

On directing effective home videos.

A108   "Bernie Balmuth Holds Fourth A.C.E. Screening Seminar." <u>American CinemaEditor</u> (Winter/Spring 1983/1984) p. 24.

The text of Wise's talk as guest speaker on February 3, 1984.

A109   Champlin, Charles. "Editing: The Splice of Life." <u>Los Angeles Times</u> (February 2, 1984).

Article on and interview with Wise and editor William Hornbeck.

A110   Williams, Rone. "UCSB Film Studies Dept. Sponsors Visit From Director Robert Wise." <u>Santa Barbara News and Review</u> (July 5, 1984).

A111   Woodard, Josef. "50 Years in Hollywood." <u>Santa Barbara News and Review</u> (July 5-July 15, 1984).

Career article and interview.

A112   Knight, Arthur. "Knight of the Movies." (column). <u>Hollywood Reporter</u> (April 12, 1985).

An interview with Wise on Princess Line's Celebrity Cruise.

A113   "Interview." <u>Cinema</u> (Paris) #322, (25 September/1 October, 1985) p. 3.

Career interview.

A114   Van Gelder, Lawrence. "At The Movies." (column). <u>The New York Times</u> (May 16, 1986).

Wise on the "mentoring" of Emilio Estevez in the latter's directorial debut <u>Wisdom</u> (1986).

A115   "Robert Wise." La Revue Du Cinema #426 (Avril, 1987) pp. 65-76.

Career interview and filmography.

A116   "Four People Award UCLA's Highest Honor." (The Summer Bruin [UCLA] June 27, 1988.

Wise receives the UCLA Medal along with Rufino Tamayo, Robert Vosper and Frank Press.

A117   Tusher, Will. "Tel Aviv U Makes a Wise Move." (Variety January 23, 1989).

Article concerning Wise's honorary fellowship on the faculty of Tel Aviv University.

A118   Christy, George. "The Great Life." (column) Hollywood Reporter (January 31, 1989).

On a tribute to Wise at the Beverly Hilton Hotel.

A119   Champlin, Charles. "Robert Wise Speaks Passionately From the Rooftops." Los Angeles Times (March 23, 1989).

A120   Mietus, Jim. "East Side Story." (Bam March 24, 1989).

Interview with Wise upon the release of Rooftops.

A121   McBride, Joseph. "Wise Raises the Rooftops After 10-Year Layoff From Directing." Daily Variety (March 28, 1989).

A122   Snow, Shauna. "Five To Receive the First Los Angeles Honors for Lifetime Arts Achievement." (Los Angeles Times November 9, 1989).

The prestigious award was presented to Wise, Eli Broad, Gordon Davidson, Ernest Fleischmann and Bella Lewitzky.

A123   Asherman, Alan. "The Man Who Was Klaatu...Michael

Rennie." (Filmfax #17, November, 1989 pp. 74-79).

A companion article to the <u>Day The Earth Stood Still</u> feature in the same issue (see below). Asherman offers an overview of Rennie's career. Although the actor was versatile, Asherman writes that the role in Wise's film "remained inexorably linked in the minds of the public and those who controlled Hollywood film casting." Asherman says that for the remainder of Rennie's career he was cast as "saintly or mysterious characters."

A124   Taylor, Al and Finch, Doug. "Director Robert Wise Remembers <u>The Day The Earth Stood Still</u>." (Filmfax #17, November, 1989 pp. 70-75).

A125   McBride, Joseph. "Directors Looks to Spook Colorizers Via <u>Haunting</u>." (<u>Variety</u>, April 25, 1990, p. 20).

In January, 1990, Wise, representing the Directors Guild of America, toured Color Systems Technology (CST) in Marina Del Ray, and was shocked to find that <u>The Haunting</u>, in which he had part ownership, had already been colorized. CST president Buddy Young said that the film "just happened to be up on the machine" when Wise came through. The director expressed his "strenuous disapproval" even though he was assured that CST had "tried to do a good job" colorizing <u>The Haunting</u>. "I don't care how good a job they do," Wise said, "you can't get the texture and tone in color. No matter how low-key it is, it's not the same as good, rich, stark black and white." [see A127 and A128 for more]

A126   Slate, Libby. "25th Anniversary for Oscar Laden <u>The Sound of Music</u>." <u>Los Angeles Times</u> (March 31, 1990).

A127   McBride, Joseph. "Wise Film To Haunt Colorizers." (<u>Variety</u> April 18, 1990).

On the thwarting of those who would colorize <u>The Haunting</u>. For more information see filmography entry on <u>The Haunting</u> and <u>Variety</u> entry by David Robb below.

A128   Robb, David. "'Haunting' Thrown Out The 'Window'."
            (Variety May 9, 1990).

When Turner Entertainment Company (TEC) announced
plans to computer color The Haunting, Wise threatened
to bring suit against the company, pointing out that his
contract stipulated that the original film was to be made
only in black and white. Further, Wise claimed that
colorization would constitute a "remake or new version"
which could not, according to the contract, be
accomplished without Wise's assent. But a Supreme
Court ruling in the Rear Window copyright case put a
stop to the colorizers plans for good. The copyright
holder of Rear Window had sued when the film was re-
released without his consent. TEC became concerned
that the heirs of Haunting author Shirley Jackson, who
held literary rights to her 1959 book "The Haunting of
Hill House" might be similarly troublesome. The legal
wranglings kept The Haunting out of circulation for
about three years. A 35mm print was shown at the
American Cinematheque's tribute to Wise in the
Summer of 1993. In December, 1993 a letterboxed -
and black and white - laser disc of The Haunting was
released by M-G-M Home video.

A129   "Still One of Our Favorite Things; The Sound of Music
            Cast Returns For a 25th Anniversary Von Trapp
            Reunion." People (September 10, 1990).

A130   McBride, Joseph. "Wise Move Raises 'Kane' For
            Viewers." (Daily Variety May 1, 1991).

In honor of the fiftieth anniversary of the original release
of Orson Welles' Citizen Kane, the film was re-released
by Paramount and Turner Entertainment in sixteen new
prints timed by Wise, Kane's original editor. As this
feature story reports, there was only so much Wise and
Kane's restorers could do to match the visual grandeur
of the original; the camera negative was destroyed in
a vault fire in the 1970s and the re-release prints had
to be made from a dupe negative struck from a 1940s-

era fine grain. McBride writes that Wise was the logical person to oversee Citizen Kane's restoration: "I'm the only one around from the technical side who remembers what it was," Wise said sadly.

A131   Bansak, Ed. "Fearing the Dark: The Val Lewton Legacy [The Robert Wise Films Part One]." Midnight Marquee #42 (Summer, 1991).

Analytical article that concentrates on Curse of the Cat People. The author points out interesting parallels between Wise and fellow Lewton alumnus Mark Robson, drawing attention to the similar kinds of films they directed over the course of their careers. But, Bansak writes, "However similar their careers may have been, one thing is certain: out of the three Lewton directors (Tourneur included), Robert Wise was the one to achieve the greatest heights of critical and public acclaim."

A132   Bansak, Ed. "Fearing the Dark: The Val Lewton Legacy [The Robert Wise Films Part Two]." Midnight Marquee #43 (Winter, 1992).

Follow-up article concentrating on The Body Snatcher.

A133   McBride, Joseph. "Wise Lauded At Eastman Gala." (Daily Variety November 14, 1991).

On the occasion of Wise's receipt of the Fifth Annual Eastman Second Century Award from Eastman Kodak. In her introductory remarks, American Film Institute Director Jean Firstenberg said, "[Wise] has devoted his life to supporting the next generation of filmmakers. In this world where there is so much ego and so much hyperbole, Bob Wise leads because he has dignified his profession."

A134   McBride, Joseph. "Wise Advice Helps Indie Holocaust Film." (Variety April 10, 1992).

The article concerns Wise's assistance on I Remember, an independently produced holocaust documentary

written by Lucy Deutsch, directed by Sara Lou
O'Connor and produced by O'Connor and Anthony O.
Ross.

A135   Thompson, Frank. "The Haunting." Apprise (October,
            1992).

            A retrospective review of the video version of Wise's
            ghost film, based in part on the author's interview with
            the director. See filmography entry on The Haunting for
            extensive excerpts from that interview.

A136   Kutner, C. Jerry. "Robert Wise, Part One: The Noir
            Years." Bright Lights (July, 1993) pp. 24-30.

            Interview in which Wise discusses his career from its
            beginnings to Odds Against Tomorrow (1959).

A137   Kutner, C. Jerry. "Robert Wise, Part Two: Life at the
            Top." Bright Lights (October, 1993) pp. 30-36.

            A continuation of the career interview in which Wise
            talks about West Side Story, The Haunting, The Sand
            Pebbles, among others, and discusses a movie he wants
            to make: "It's the real story of a horse who was born
            on a stud farm in northern Poland just before the start
            of World War II. And it tells the story through the war
            with the local people and the partisans and the Russians
            coming in and going, the Germans coming in, taking
            over the stud farms. And eventually he and these other
            horses are shipped to a farm in Czechoslovakia near the
            Austrian border. And he's a fine character. I'd shoot the
            whole thing over in Poland. Make a hell of a movie!"

A138   Morrell, David. "The Major and the Minor McQueen."
            The Perfect Vision Volume 5, Number 20 (Winter,
            1994).

            A review of the Sand Pebbles laser disc.

A139   "Robert Wise: On McQueen and The Sand Pebbles."
            The Perfect Vision Volume 5, Number 20 (Winter,

Sidebar to A138 in which Wise discusses Steve McQueen and the production of The Sand Pebbles.

A140 "Robert Wise." The Perfect Vision Volume 5, Number 20 (Winter, 1994).

Interview concentrating on Wise's contributions to film noir, including Born to Kill, The Set-Up, and the Val Lewton movies at RKO.

A141 "Simone Simon." The Perfect Vision Volume 5, Number 20 (Winter, 1994).

Interview with the star of Curse of the Cat People in which she discusses working with Wise and Val Lewton.

A142 Sarris, Andrew. "Val Lewton: RKO's Prince of Darkness." The Perfect Vision Volume 5, Number 20 (Winter, 1994).

Perceptive essay by the eminent film critic on Lewton's unique legacy of subtle horror.

Books

B1 Aylesworth, Thomas G. Broadway To Hollywood. New York: Gallery Books, 1985.

An attractive, lushly illustrated survey of Broadway musicals which have been adapted to the screen. Wise's West Side Story and The Sound of Music are among the productions so treated.

B2   Basinger, Jeanine. <u>A Woman's View: How Hollywood Spoke to Women 1930-1960</u>. New York: Alfred A. Knopf, Inc., 1993.

          Superb examination of the treatment of women in American film contains an essay on <u>Three Secrets</u>.

B3   Bergan, Ronald, Graham Fuller and David Malcolm. <u>Academy Award Winners</u>. New York: Crescent Books, 1986.

          Entries on <u>The Sound of Music</u> and <u>West Side Story</u>.

B4   Bergan, Ronald. <u>The United Artists Story</u>. New York: Crown Publishers, Inc., 1986.

          Each United Artists film - including every film which Robert Wise produced and/or directed for the company - is discussed and evaluated in this large format studio history.

B5   Bergman, Ronald. <u>A - Z of Movie Direction</u>. London and New York: Proteus, 1982.

          Career article.

B6   Biskind, Peter. <u>Seeing Is Believing</u>. New York: Pantheon Books, 1983.

          A witty and intelligent meditation on the films of the 1950s. Includes in-depth discussions of <u>The Day The Earth Stood Still</u> and <u>Executive Suite</u>.

B7   Bojarski, Richard and Kenneth Beale. <u>The Films of Boris Karloff</u>. Secaucus, New Jersey: The Citadel Press, 1974.

          Typical Citadel "Films Of..." entry offers credits, synopsis and a sampling of contemporary reviews of each Karloff film, including Wise's <u>The Body Snatcher</u>.

B8   Bojarski, Richard. <u>The Films of Bela Lugosi</u>. Secaucus, New Jersey: The Citadel Press, 1980. see: <u>The Films</u>

of Boris Karloff above.

B9   Bookbinder, Robert. The Films of the Seventies.
            Secaucus, New Jersey: Citadel Press, 1982.

            Chapter on Star Trek -- The Motion Picture.

B10   Bowser, Eileen, ed. Film Notes. New York: The Museum
            of Modern Art, 1969.

            A collection of program notes for films screened at New
            York's Museum of Modern Art. Editor Eileen Bowser
            contributes an insightful essay on Wise's The Set-Up:
            "... an extraordinary film. This is more than an expose
            of boxing: it is, quite unpretentiously, a statement of
            the human condition."

B11   Brode, Douglas. The Films of the Sixties. Secaucus,
            New Jersey: Citadel Press, 1980.

            Chapters on West Side Story and The Sound of Music.

B12   Brosnan, John. The Horror People. New York:
            St. Martin's Press, 1976.

            A collection of essays on the stars, writers and
            filmmakers behind the great horror films. The book
            includes some discussion about Wise's horror films and
            a brief biographical sketch of Wise, as well as some
            minor interview quotes.

B13   Carr, Robert E. and Hayes, R.M. Wide Screen Movies:
            A History and Filmography of Wide Gauge Filmmaking.
            Jefferson, North Carolina, and London: McFarland and
            Company, Inc., Publishers, 1988.

            Lengthy credits and brief notes on Wise's 70mm films
            The Sound of Music, West Side Story, and Star!.

B14   Cary, John, Spectacular: The Story of Epic Films.
            Secaucus, New Jersey: Castle Books, 1974.

            This study of epic movies contains a chapter, "The

Making of an Epic," on Wise's <u>Helen of Troy</u>. In addition
to some background information, stills, conceptual art
and costume sketches, the chapter also contains a
lengthy interview with Wise and continuity artist
Maurice Zuberano.

B15   Charnez, Casey St.   <u>The Films of Steve McQueen</u>.
         Secaucus, New Jersey: The Citadel Press, 1984.

         Credits, synopses and reviews of each of McQueen's
         films including Wise's <u>The Sand Pebbles</u>.

B16   Clarens, Carlos. <u>An Illustrated History of the Horror
         Film</u>. New York: G.P. Putnam's Sons, 1967.

         Sensitive and comprehensive overview of horror films
         includes discussion of Wise's <u>The Body Snatcher</u>, <u>Curse
         of the Cat People</u>, <u>The Day The Earth Stood Still</u>, and
         <u>The Haunting</u>.

B17   Clinch, Minty. <u>Burt Lancaster</u>. New York: Stein and Day
         Publishers, 1984.

B18   Colomina, Beatriz, ed. <u>Sexuality and Space</u>. Princeton,
         New Jersey: Princeton Architectural Press, 1992.

         Chapter, "Female Spectator, Lesbian Specter: <u>The
         Haunting</u>" by Patricia White. The author finds that
         Hollywood's best "serious" ghost movies - <u>Curse of the
         Cat People</u> (1944), <u>The Uninvited</u> (1944), <u>The
         Innocents</u> (1961) and <u>The Haunting</u> (1963) - all "by
         some uncanny coincidence" contain lesbian overtones.
         White argues persuasively in this lengthy, intriguing
         reading of Wise's film that <u>The Haunting</u> is "one of the
         screen's most spine-tingling representations of the
         disruptive force of lesbian desire."

B19   Cottrell, John. <u>Julie Andrews: The Unauthorized Life
         Story of A Super-Star</u>. New York: Dell Publishing
         Company, Inc., 1968.

         Insubstantial fluff biography of Andrews with some
         information about, but little insight into, her films with

Wise: The Sound of Music and Star!.

B20   Coursodon, Jean-Pierre and Pierre Sauvage. American Directors Volume II. New York: McGraw-Hill Book Company, 1983.

A lengthy (eleven page), in-depth, generally unfavorable, critical analysis of Wise's work: "Wise's versatility is impressive (he has made films in practically every known genre), but it is mere versatility; no unifying vision underlies it."

B21   Crowther, Bosley. Re-runs: Fifty Memorable Films. New York: G. P. Putnam's Sons, 1978.

In this follow-up to Vintage Films (1977; B22), Crowther writes appreciatively of West Side Story.

B22   Crowther, Bosley. Vintage Films. New York: G. P. Putnam's Sons, 1977.

A book of essays on memorable movies. Wise's contribution to The Magnificent Ambersons is considered in the chapter on that film.

B23   Dorian, Bob. Bob Dorian's Classic Movies. Holbrook, Massachusetts: Bob Adams Publishers Inc., 1990.

Dorian, best known as a host on the American Movie Classics cable channel, compiled this book of brief, general essays, including one on Wise's The Day The Earth Stood Still.

B24   Douglas, Drake. Horrors!. Woodstock, New York: The Overlook Press, 1989.

Somewhat superficial overview of horror in film and literature mentions much of Wise's horror work in passing. The Body Snatcher is discussed in some detail on pp. 263-265.

B25   Eames, John Douglas. The M-G-M Story: The Complete History of Fifty Roaring Years. New York: Crown

Publishers, 1975.

The first, and least informative, of the series of large format studio histories. The entries are brief and tend to be superficial. Each of Wise's M-G-M films is discussed.

B26   Eames, John Douglas. The Paramount Story. New York: Crown Publishers, Inc., 1985.

The more attentive to detail than Eames' previous The M-G-M Story; unfortunately, Wise only made one film for Paramount: Star Trek -- the Motion Picture.

B27   Edmonds, I. G. and Reiko Mimura. The Oscar Directors. London: The Tantivy Press, 1980.

Chapters on The Sound of Music and West Side Story.

B28   Eells, George and Stanley Musgrove. Mae West: A Biography. New York: William Morrow and Company Inc., 1982.

This biography of the venerable star contains some discussion on the unproduced television special which West and Wise worked on in the late 60s. West says of her producer, "Going from Julie Andrews to Mae West -- he's certainly versatile!"

B29   Erens, Patricia. The Films of Shirley MacLaine. South Brunswick and New York: A. S. Barnes and Company, 1978.

Film-by-film survey of MacLaine's career including Two For The Seesaw.

B30   Everman, Welch, Cult Horror Films. Secaucus New Jersey: The Citadel Press, 1993.

Superficial coverage of many horror films, with a tendency toward the cheesy (Plan 9 From Outer Space). Wise's Audrey Rose is the subject of one chapter but, aside from a plot synopsis and a few photographs, it contains little of note.

B31   Everson, William K. <u>Classics of the Horror Film</u>.
       Secaucus, New Jersey: The Citadel Press, 1974.

       Admirably thorough and delightfully informal musings
       on the horror film from the film scholar who has seen
       everything. Included are extended discussions of Wise's
       <u>The Body Snatcher</u> ("one of the most literate and
       restrained of all horror films"), <u>Curse of the Cat People</u>,
       and <u>The Haunting</u> ("the most elaborate and ambitious
       of all movie ghost stories").

B32   Everson, William K. <u>A Pictorial History of the Western
       Film</u>. Secaucus, New Jersey: The Citadel Press, 1969.

       Excellent overview of Westerns with brief mention of
       Wise's <u>Blood on the Moon</u>.

B33   Everson, William K. and Fenin, George N. <u>The Western</u>.
       New York: Grossman Publishers, 1973. (Revision of
       1962 edition).

       Wise's <u>Tribute to a Bad Man</u> is discussed in this
       comprehensive survey of Western films.

B34   Fury, David. <u>The Cinema of Burt Lancaster</u>.
       Minneapolis: Stanton Pub. Services/Artist's Press,
       1989.

B35   Grivel, Daniele and Roland Lacourbe. <u>Robert Wise:
       Filmo-11</u>. Paris: Edilg, 1985.

       Part of a critical and biographical series on filmmakers,
       this is the first book-length study of Wise's career to
       reach print.

B36   Gross, Edward and Kay Anderson, Wendy Rathbone,
       Ron Magid, Sheldon Teitelbaum. <u>The Making of the
       Trek Films</u>. New York: Image Publishing, 1991.

       Includes interview with Wise conducted by Randy and
       Jean Marc Lofficier.

B37   Halliwell, Leslie. <u>Halliwell's Filmgoer's and Video
           Viewer's Companion: Ninth Edition</u>. New York:
           Perennial Library, 1990.

           Brief, but engaging, entries on films, filmmakers and all
           related subjects. Wise is represented by a list of his
           films and several of his most notable movies: <u>The Body
           Snatcher</u>, <u>Executive Suite</u>, <u>West Side Story</u>, <u>The Sound
           of Music</u>, <u>Star!</u> - are given concise reviews. Halliwell,
           who died in 1989, regularly updated this volume, which
           first appeared in 1965. A handy, essential movie
           reference book.

B38   Hardy, Phil. <u>The Encyclopedia of Horror Movies</u>. New
           York: Harper and Row, Publishers, 1986.

           Excellent discussions of Wise's horror films: <u>Audrey
           Rose</u> ("solidly crafted by Wise and mercifully free of
           special effects trickery"), <u>The Body Snatcher</u> ("superbly
           controlled and strikingly literate"), <u>Curse of the Cat
           People</u> ("a marvelous little film"), <u>A Game of Death</u>
           ("lacks the controlled intensity of [<u>The Most Dangerous
           Game</u>]"), and <u>The Haunting</u> ("a ponderous affair").

B39   Hardy, Phil, ed. <u>The Film Encyclopedia: Science Fiction</u>.
           New York: William Morrow and Company, Inc., 1982.

           Essays on Wise's science fiction films, <u>The Day
           The Earth Stood Still</u> and <u>Star Trek -- The Motion
           Picture</u>.

B40   Hardy, Phil. <u>The Film Encyclopedia: Western Movies</u>.
           New York: William Morrow and Company, Inc., 1983.

           Knowledgable entries on Wise's westerns: <u>Blood on the
           Moon</u> ("taut"), <u>Two Flags West</u> "ambitious [and]
           energetic"), and <u>Tribute to a Bad Man</u> ("Beautifully
           photographed...intriguing little Western").

B41   Higham, Charles. <u>Celebrity Circus</u>. New York, Delacorte
           Press, 1979.

           A collection of interviews with stars, directors and other

vivid personalities. Wise is represented by a 1968 interview in which he talks about his career with some stress upon I Want To Live! and Star!. There is also a 1977 interview with Julie Andrews in which the subjects of The Sound of Music and Star! are broached.

B42   Hirschhorn, Clive. The Hollywood Musical. New York: Crown Publishers, Inc., 1981.

             Like the other large format studio histories in this series (see also The United Artists Story, The M-G-M Story, etc.) this book attempts to pack a great deal of information in short, tightly written entries. Each of Wise's musicals is discussed here.

B43   Hirschhorn, Clive. The Warner Bros. Story. New York: Crown Publishers, Inc., 1979.

             Wise's three features for Warner Bros. - Three Secrets, So Big, and Helen of Troy - are concisely and individually treated in this large format studio history.

B44   Hirschhorn, Clive. The Universal Story. New York: Crown Publishers, Inc., 1983.

             Hirschhorn discusses - and dismisses - each of the three films Wise directed at Universal: The Andromeda Strain, Two People, and The Hindenburg.

B45   Hogan, David J. Dark Romance: Sexuality in the Horror Film. Jefferson, North Carolina and London: McFarland and Company Inc., Publishers, 1983.

             Contains a brief discussion of the sexual themes in The Haunting.

B46   Jewell, Richard B. and Vernon Harbin. The RKO Story. New York: Arlington House, 1982.

             Film-by-film survey of the output of RKO Studios. Each of the RKO films on which Wise worked as editor or director is discussed here. Every entry contains principle credits, a brief synopsis, some background detail and critical response.

B47   Kael, Pauline The Citizen Kane Book. Boston, Toronto:
       Little, Brown and Company, 1971.

       The influential critic's controversial attempt to treat
       screenwriter Herman J. Mankiewicz as the key creative
       mind behind Orson Welles' Citizen Kane. Kael's essay
       "Raising Kane," which first appeared in The New
       Yorker, discusses the film's production and touches
       briefly on Wise's contributions as editor.

B48   Katz, Ephraim. The Film Encyclopedia. New York:
       Harper and Row Publishers, Inc., 1979.

       The single most valuable motion picture reference book,
       filled with insightful critical and biographical essays
       and thorough film listings. While the thrust of the book
       is primarily biographical, Katz also offers knowledgable
       entries on film techniques, genres, tools and related
       subjects. Wise and most of his prominent co-workers
       are represented. Katz worked on a much-needed update
       of the book until his death in 1992. His work was
       completed by others and this welcome volume was
       published in 1994.

B49   Leyda, Jay, ed. Voices of Film Experience 1894 to the
       Present. New York: Macmillan Publishing Company,
       Inc., 1977.

       In this excellent oral history compilation Wise discusses
       The Magnificent Ambersons, co-directing West Side
       Story and how beginning as an editor influenced his
       work as a director.

B50   Leaming, Barbara. Orson Welles. New York: Viking
       Penguin Inc., 1985.

       Wise was interviewed for this compelling biography in
       which his contributions as editor to Citizen Kane and
       The Magnificent Ambersons are discussed.

B51   Lindsay, Cynthia. Dear Boris. New York: Alfred A.

Knopf, 1975.

Uncritical and affectionate biography of Boris Karloff. Wise is briefly quoted on his first meeting with Karloff, though the excellent film they made together -- The Body Snatcher -- is mentioned only in passing.

B52   Lyon, Christopher. The International Dictionary of Films and Filmmakers: Volume II "Directors/Filmmakers." Chicago and London: St. James Press Inc., 1984.

Wise essay, filmography and bibliography. Essay, entirely lacking a critical stance, was written by DeWitt Bodeen, screenwriter for Wise's Curse of the Cat People.

B53   Maltin, Leonard, et al. Leonard Maltin's Movie and Video Guide. New York: Signet Books, 1994.

Maltin and his crew annually update this vital reference volume in which virtually every feature film licensed for television distribution is evaluated (using a star system). Maltin packs an impressive amount of information into each brief entry, including plot points, production information, major credits, running time, home video availability and more. Beginning in the 1994 edition (published in September, 1993) Maltin added the extremely valuable designation of which films were originally filmed in a widescreen format, which can warn a viewer off watching a panned-and-scanned The Haunting or West Side Story.

B54   Marill, Alvin H. Robert Mitchum on the Screen. South Brunswick and New York: A.S. Barnes and Company, 1978.

Film-by-film coverage of Mitchum's career includes credits, synopsis and critical response to Blood on the Moon and Two For The Seesaw.

B55   Moreno, Eduardo. The Films of Susan Hayward. Secaucus, New Jersey: Citadel Press, 1979.

Credits, synopsis and reviews of I Want To Live!.

B56   Osborne, Robert. Academy Awards Illustrated. La Habra: Ernest E. Schwork, 1966.

The Wise material in this overview of the Academy Awards focuses on The Sound of Music and West Side Story.

B57   Parrish, Robert. Growing Up In Hollywood. New York and London: Harcourt Brace Jovanovich, 1976.

The author, an editor, director and actor, mentions his friend Wise in passing several times in this amusing memoir of a life in Hollywood.

B58   Peary, Danny. Close-Ups: The Movie Star Book. New York: The Workman Publishing Company, Inc., 1978.

In this book of appreciative essays on movie stars, Wise contributes a warm chapter on his work with Susan Hayward on I Want To Live!, writing, "In my mind she was one of the most professional actresses with whom I have worked, willing to explore her capabilities in order to give the best performance she could, and responsive to me and the other actors."

B59   Roud, Richard, ed. Cinema: A Critical Dictionary -- The Major Film-makers. Volume Two: Kinugasa to Zanussi. New York: The Viking Press, 1980.

The Wise essay, by John Russell Taylor, is among the book's briefest, but Taylor finds much in Wise's cinema to admire, calling the director the epitome of the "stunningly capable Hollywood craftsman who can turn his hand successfully to almost any genre."

B60   Sackett, Susan. The Making of "Star Trek - The Motion Picture". New Jersey: A Wallaby Book Published by Pocket Books, 1980.

B61   Sarris, Andrew. The American Cinema: Directors and Directions 1929-1968. New York: E.P. Dutton and

Company, Inc., 1968.

Influential overview of American directors includes Wise under the category "Strained Seriousness." Sarris complains that "the stylistic signature of Robert Wise is indistinct to the point of invisibility."

B62   Schary, Dore. Heyday. New York: Little, Brown, 1979.

Veteran producer Schary briefly discusses the projects on which he worked with Wise and recounts an encounter with James Dean, who was originally cast as Rocky Graziano in Somebody Up There Likes Me.

B63   Sennett, Ted. Great Movie Directors. New York: Harry N. Abrams, Inc., 1986.

Biographical entry.

B64   Shales, Tom, etc. The American Film Heritage: Impressions From The American Film Institute Archives. Washington, D.C.: Acropolis Books Ltd., 1972.

Excellent compilation of essays by several authors and film historians on personalities, genres and specific films. Joel E. Siegel, author of Val Lewton: The Reality of Terror, contributes a chapter on Lewton whose "distinctive identity shaped the films he produced, and whose artistic guidance launched subsequently celebrated directors like Robert Wise on their own careers."

B65   Siegel, Joel E. Val Lewton: The Reality of Terror. New York: The Viking Press, 1973.

Excellent history of Val Lewton's low-budget unit at RKO and insightful analysis of the films made there make this an indispensable volume. Wise's work for and with Lewton is thoroughly examined. Wise, and other Lewton friends and co-workers, were interviewed for this book and quoted at length.

B66   Siegel, Scott and Barbara. The Encyclopedia of
            Hollywood. New York, Oxford, Sydney: Facts on File,
            1990.

            Biographical entry.

B67   Silver, Alain and Elizabeth Ward, eds. Film Noir.
            Woodstock, New York: The Overlook Press, 1979.

            A collection of writings on film noir contains perceptive
            comments on Wise's many contributions to the genre:
            Born To Kill, The Captive City, House on Telegraph Hill,
            Odds Against Tomorrow, and The Set-Up.

B68   Silverman, Stephen. The Fox That Got Away.
            Secaucus, New Jersey: Lyle Stuart, Inc., 1988.

            A history of 20th Century-Fox.

B69   Sinyard, Neil. Classic Movies. Salem, New Hampshire:
            Salem House, 1985.

            Essay on The Sound of Music.

B70   Smith, Ella. Starring Miss Barbara Stanwyck. New York:
            Crown Publishers, Inc., 1974.

            In this excellent critical biography, Wise discusses
            working with Stanwyck on Executive Suite.

B71   Smith, Steven C. A Heart At Fire's Center: The Life and
            Music of Bernard Herrmann. Berkeley, Los Angeles,
            Oxford: University of California Press, 1991.

            In this thorough biography of composer Herrmann, Wise
            is quoted on working with Herrmann on the films Citizen
            Kane, The Magnificent Ambersons, and The Day The
            Earth Stood Still. He also tells of how a low budget
            kept Herrmann from composing the score to Captive
            City.

B72   Spindle, Les. Julie Andrews: A Bio-Bibliography.
            Westport, Connecticut: Greenwood Press, 1989.

B73   Sullivan, Jack, ed. The Penguin Encyclopedia of
             Horror and the Supernatural. New York: Viking Penguin
             Inc., 1986.

             This encyclopedia covers horror and the supernatural in
             film, literature, art, music and other media. It contains
             a fine biographical essay on Wise by John Calhoun and
             critical entries on the following Wise films: The Body
             Snatcher and Curse of the Cat People (essays by
             Timothy Sullivan); and The Haunting (essay by Kim
             Newman).

B74   Telotte, J.P. Dreams of Darkness: Fantasy and the Films
             of Val Lewton. Urbana and Chicago: University of
             Illinois Press, 1985.

             Serious, scholarly analysis of the Lewton horror films.

B75   Terrill, Marshall. Steve McQueen: Portrait of an
             American Rebel. New York: Donald I. Fine, Inc., 1993.

             Thorough biography of McQueen features chapter, with
             quotes from Wise, on the making of The Sand Pebbles
             and information on McQueen's screen debut in
             Somebody Up There Likes Me.

B76   Thomson, David. A Biographical Dictionary of Film. New
             York: William Morrow and Company, Inc., 1976.

             A brief, rather unfavorable, analysis of Wise's career in
             which Thomson complains that "...his better credits are
             only the haphazard products of artistic aimlessness
             given rare guidance." Thomson calls The Sound of
             Music "appalling," The Set-Up "over-rated" and The
             Haunting "muddled [and] tentative."

B77   Van Hise, James. Trek: The Making of the Movies. Las
             Vegas, Nevada: Pioneer Books, Inc., 1992.

B78   Von Trapp, Maria. Maria-My Own Story. Carol Stream,
             Illinois: Creation House, 1972.

B79   Webb, Michael, ed. Hollywood: Legend and Reality.
             Boston: Little, Brown and Company, 1986.

             The catalog of a major museum exhibition on art
             direction and design in the movies, the book is itself
             lavishly and beautifully designed and illustrated.
             Included in the text is a letter from West Side Story
             production designer Boris Leven to Wise on Leven's
             ideas regarding the "look" of that film.

B80   Weldon, Michael. The Psychotronic Encyclopedia of
             Film. New York: Ballantine Books, 1983.

             Terse, sometimes hilarious, entries on films which. says
             the author, are "often treated with indifference or
             contempt by other movie guides." Wise's horror and
             science fiction films are considered: The Andromeda
             Strain ("an excellent big-budget technological thriller"),
             Audrey Rose, The Body Snatcher, Curse of the Cat
             People ("a sensitive classic"), The Day the Earth Stood
             Still, A Game of Death, The Haunting ("undoubtedly the
             scariest ghost movie ever made").

B81   Wiley, Mason and Damien Bona. Inside Oscar: The
             Unofficial History of the Academy Awards. New York:
             Ballantine Books, 1986. Revised and updated, 1993.

             This book, "neither authorized nor endorsed by the
             Academy of Motion Picture Arts and Sciences," is a
             witty, gossipy history of the Oscars. Wise and his films
             are the subjects of several anecdotes.

B82   Willis, Donald, ed. Variety's Complete Science Fiction
             Reviews. New York and London: Garland Publishing,
             Inc., 1985.

             A compilation of reviews which first appeared in
             Variety, the "Show Business Bible." Wise films include
             The Day The Earth Stood Still and Star Trek - The
             Motion Picture.

B83   Windeler, Robert. Julie Andrews - A Biography. New
             York: St. Martin Press, 1983.

B84   Wood, Bret. _Orson Welles: A Bio-Bibliography_. Westport, Connecticut: Greenwood Press, 1990.

The best, most comprehensive of Greenwood's Bio-Bibliography series.

B85   Wyler, William and Axel Madsen. _William Wyler -The Authorized Biography_. New York: Thomas Y. Crowell Company, 1973.

This interesting memoir touches on Wyler's connection to _The Sound of Music_.

Unrealized Projects

U1   <u>Battle</u>, a biography of famed war photographer Robert Capa. This was supposed to be Wise's first project for the Mirisch company, for which he made <u>West Side Story</u> instead. 1960.

U2   <u>The Bobbsey Twins</u>, based on the popular children's book series by Laura Lee Hope. The script was to have been written by Allen Vincent, with songs by Sammy Fain and Paul Francis Webster. Veteran writer Frances Marion was to be story consultant. Wise planned to develop the idea into a television series after the feature film was completed. 1965.

U3   <u>A Spy in the House of Love</u> from the novel by Anais Nin. 1966.

U4   <u>An Evening with Mae West</u>, a television special to have been produced by Wise. After several months' planning -- and little network interest -- the program was abandoned. 1968.

U5   <u>Craig and Joan</u> from Eliot Asinof's book about two teenagers who form a suicide pact for peace. 1970.

U6   <u>The Old Man</u> a drama about abolitionist John Brown, from the book by Truman Nelson, with a script by

Michael Wilson. A <u>New York Times</u> article (March 31, 1974) quotes Wise on the subject of Raymond Massey, who had already portrayed John Brown in two films: "We feel John Brown hasn't really been done in films and that this book presents him as an extraordinary man, as a fascinating, sometimes misunderstood early American character and as a historic figure with an amazingly fine, creative mind." 1976.

U7   <u>The House on Garibaldi Street</u>, the story of Nazi war criminal Adolph Eichmann's capture in Argentina, where he lived in hiding after World War II. Wise called it "a real life caper, and a fascinating one." 1977. The film was eventually made as a television movie in 1979, directed by Peter Collinson and starring Topol and Martin Balsam.

U8   <u>Time and Again</u>, based upon the novel by Jack Finney. "It's a period piece," Wise told John Gallagher in 1977, "a study of time travel; an unusual subject but marvelously done. It's a very, very expensive picture because it means recreating New York of the late 1880's. The studios we took it to felt there wasn't enough action and excitement and pizazz to justify a budget of 12 to 14 million. It's a project that other people have been interested in around town and have optioned over the years but nobody's been able successfully to get it on the screen." [A85] ca. 1970s.

U9   <u>High Times Hard Times</u>, the life of jazz singer Anita O'Day. 1985.

U10   <u>Mae West</u> to star Bette Midler. 1985.

U11   <u>Zorba The Greek</u>. A musical based on the classic film and a subsequent musical play. Anthony Quinn was to repeat his role from the original. Wise remembered, "Saul Chaplin was going to be the musical director, Michael Kidd the choreographer and Ernest Lehman was going to write the script. John Travolta was supposed to co-star. We were working with a company that wasn't doing too well. At the beginning of pre-

production, their stock was high and we had a good
budget and all their support. But after a few months,
their stock fell and they started cutting back on us so
much that we finally decided to chuck it. Too bad. We
were really excited by the project." [Interview with
Frank Thompson, March 9, 1994] ca. 1980s.

Film Title Index

The letter-number combinations in the index refer to the categories in which the references may be found. For instance, when *Alice Adams* is followed by F3, that means that the reader should go to the third entry in the Filmography section. Bibliography references for articles will be found under A and books under B. The letter U refers to Wise's unrealized projects.

Name Index

The letter-number combinations in the index refer to the categories in which the references may be found. For instance, when Julie Andrews' name is followed by B19, that means the reader should go to the nineteenth entry in the "Books" section of the Bibliography. Bibliography references for articles will be found under A and Filmography entries under F. The letter U refers to Wise's unrealized projects.

About the Author

FRANK THOMPSON is a writer and film historian. His books include *Tim Burton's "The Nightmare Before Christmas"* (1993), *Alamo Movies* (1994), and *Henry King* (1995). He has also written television scripts including *Frank Capra: A Personal Remembrance* (1992), film scripts such as *The Last Stand* (1994), and many articles for professional journals and magazines.

Titles in
Bio-Bibliographies in the Performing Arts

Milos Forman: A Bio-Bibliography
Thomas J. Slater

Kate Smith: A Bio-Bibliography
Michael R. Pitts

Patty Duke: A Bio-Bibliography
Stephen L. Eberly

Carole Lombard: A Bio-Bibliography
Robert D. Matzen

Eva Le Gallienne: A Bio-Bibliography
Robert A. Schanke

Julie Andrews: A Bio-Bibliography
Les Spindle

Richard Widmark: A Bio-Bibliography
Kim Holston

Orson Welles: A Bio-Bibliography
Bret Wood

Ann Sothern: A Bio-Bibliography
Margie Schultz

Alice Faye: A Bio-Bibliography
Barry Rivadue

Jennifer Jones: A Bio-Bibliography
Jeffrey L. Carrier

Cary Grant: A Bio-Bibliography
Beverley Bare Buehrer

Maureen O'Sullivan: A Bio-Bibliography
Connie J. Billips

Ava Gardner: A Bio-Bibliography
Karin J. Fowler

Jean Arthur: A Bio-Bibliography
Arthur Pierce and Douglas Swarthout

Donna Reed: A Bio-Bibliography
Brenda Scott Royce

Gordon MacRae: A Bio-Bibliography
Bruce R. Leiby

Mary Martin: A Bio-Bibliography
Barry Rivadue

Irene Dunne: A Bio-Bibliography
Margie Schultz

Anne Baxter: A Bio-Bibliography
Karin J. Fowler

Tallulah Bankhead: A Bio-Bibliography
Jeffrey L. Carrier

Jessica Tandy: A Bio-Bibliography
Milly S. Barranger

Janet Gaynor: A Bio-Bibliography
Connie Billips

James Stewart: A Bio-Bibliography
Gerard Molyneaux

Joseph Papp: A Bio-Bibliography
Barbara Lee Horn

Henry Fonda: A Bio-Bibliography
Kevin Sweeney

Edwin Booth: A Bio-Bibliography
L. Terry Oggel

Ethel Merman: A Bio-Bibliography
George B. Bryan

Lauren Bacall: A Bio-Bibliography
Brenda Scott Royce

Joseph Chaikin: A Bio-Bibliography
Alex Gildzen and Dimitris Karageorgiou

Richard Burton: A Bio-Bibliography
Tyrone Steverson

Maureen Stapleton: A Bio-Bibliography
Jeannie M. Woods

David Merrick: A Bio-Bibliography
Barbara Lee Horn

Vivien Leigh: A Bio-Bibliography
Cynthia Marylee Molt

Robert Mitchum: A Bio-Bibliography
Jerry Roberts

Agnes Moorehead: A Bio-Bibliography
Lynn Kear

www.ingramcontent.com/pod-product-compliance
Lightning Source LLC
Chambersburg PA
CBHW070443100426
42812CB00004B/1197